Designing for Pupils with Special Educational Needs Special Schools

London: HMSO

Department for Education
Sanctuary Buildings
Great Smith Street
London SW1P 3BT

Tel. 071-925 5000

The name of the Department of Education and
Science was changed to Department for Education
on 6 July 1992. However, the previous name is
retained in this publication where appropriate.

Edited by DFE Information Branch
Artwork by DFE Architects and Building
Branch
IB/1016/11/6

HMSO publications are available from:

HMSO Publications Centre
(Mail, fax and telephone orders only)
PO Box 276, London, SW8 5DT
Telephone orders 071-873 9090
General enquiries 071-873 0011
(queuing system in operation for both numbers)
Fax orders 071-873 8200

HMSO Bookshops
49 High Holborn, London, WC1V 6HB
(counter service only)
071-873 0011 Fax 071-873 8200
258 Broad Street, Birmingham, B1 2HE
021-643 3740 Fax 021-643 6510
Southey House, 33 Wine Street, Bristol, BS1 2BQ
0272 264306 Fax 0272 294515
9-21 Princess Street, Manchester, M60 8AS
061-834 7201 Fax 061-833 0634
16 Arthur Street, Belfast, BT1 4GD
0232 238451 Fax 0232 235401
71 Lothian Road, Edinburgh, EH3 9AZ
031-228 4181 Fax 031-229 2734

**HMSO's Accredited Agents
(see Yellow Pages)**

and through good booksellers

Printed in the United Kingdom for HMSO Dd 295145 C22 10/92 17647

Contents

List of figures

Key to symbols used in figures

T: teacher SSA: special support assistant TE: technician

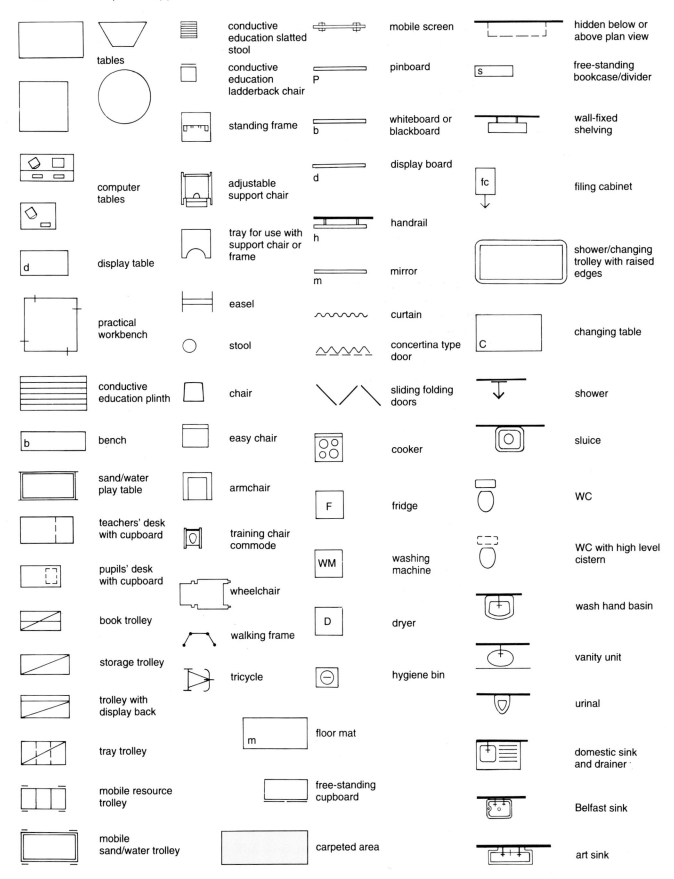

	tables
	computer tables
d	display table
	practical workbench
	conductive education plinth
b	bench
	sand/water play table
	teachers' desk with cupboard
	pupils' desk with cupboard
	book trolley
	storage trolley
	trolley with display back
	tray trolley
	mobile resource trolley
	mobile sand/water trolley

	conductive education slatted stool
	conductive education ladderback chair
	standing frame
	adjustable support chair
	tray for use with support chair or frame
	easel
	stool
	chair
	easy chair
	armchair
	training chair commode
	wheelchair
	walking frame
	tricycle
m	floor mat
	free-standing cupboard
	carpeted area

	mobile screen
P	pinboard
b	whiteboard or blackboard
d	display board
h	handrail
m	mirror
	curtain
	concertina type door
	sliding folding doors
	cooker
F	fridge
WM	washing machine
D	dryer
	hygiene bin

	hidden below or above plan view
s	free-standing bookcase/divider
	wall-fixed shelving
fc	filing cabinet
	shower/changing trolley with raised edges
C	changing table
	shower
	sluice
	WC
	WC with high level cistern
	wash hand basin
	vanity unit
	urinal
	domestic sink and drainer
	Belfast sink
	art sink

List of illustrations

List of tables

Preface

This publication considers the accommodation requirements of special schools in the light of the changing pattern of special education provision in recent years. It has been prepared by the Architects and Building (A&B) Branch of the Department for Education (DFE) in consultation with Her Majesty's Inspectorate (HMI). It draws upon information accumulated over a period of years through the monitoring of provision in England and represents a national overview of problems met at local level.

The Department wishes to thank authorities and school staff, including those in the non-maintained and independent sectors, who have contributed time, comment and advice.

It is hoped that the publication will assist LEA advisers, education officers, governing bodies, head teachers and architects in their early discussions and in the preparation of briefs.

Architects and Building Branch
September 1992

1 Introduction

1.1 National and international perspectives on the provision appropriate to pupils with special educational needs were reflected in this country in the 1978 Warnock Report[1] and the Education Act 1981. Emphasis was laid on ensuring that pupils with special educational needs had equal opportunities with other pupils, and this contributed to a changing pattern of special educational provision.

1.2 Today an increasing proportion of pupils who earlier might have been educated in special schools are taught in ordinary schools. On the average, therefore, pupils now attending special schools are those who have more severe and complex learning difficulties. The Education Reform Act 1988 requires all pupils to have access to a balanced and broadly based curriculum. This curricular requirement, coupled with the increasingly complex needs of the pupils, carries implications for accommodation in special schools.

1.3 Guidance to those involved in planning and adapting ordinary primary and secondary school buildings when pupils with special educational needs are on roll was provided in *Building Bulletin 61: Designing for Children with Special Educational Needs: Ordinary Schools*[2]. The purpose of the present document is to provide guidance for those involved in the briefing and planning of special schools.

1.4 The main educational and organisational characteristics of special schools that affect the accommodation include:

- the proportion of pupils with more complex and severe learning difficulties and disabilities. This has implications for accommodation, for levels of staffing and for aids and equipment to support their curriculum

- how and to what extent special support assistants carrying out activities in the classroom are deployed

- inter-disciplinary work in a variety of contexts, for example physiotherapists, speech and language therapists and occupational therapists working in the teaching areas

- the need to support co-operative and cross-curricular work through the provision of space to enable pupils to be grouped flexibly

- the recognition of greater parental involvement, as advocated by the Warnock Report

- the trend within local education authorities (LEAs) towards reorganisation of all-age special schools into separate primary and secondary special schools in order to provide curriculum planning and resourcing. Where this has not occurred, the development of different primary and secondary modes of organisation within the all-age school can assist such processes

- an extension of provision for students aged 16 to 19 in some special schools and the need to provide these students with a curriculum that places increased emphasis on preparation for adult life

- the implications of the National Curriculum, modified as appropriate, for provision to pursue a range of subjects and to enable staff to operate in specialist or consultant roles

- the use of information technology as part of the learning process within classrooms, for example, the use of computers, including the use of special interfaces for pupils with particular difficulties

- the additional use of some special schools as resource centres to support the teaching of pupils with special educational needs in ordinary schools, requiring accommodation for this extended role.

2 | Scope and use of the Bulletin

2.1 This document is concerned with the teaching and related accommodation in maintained special schools. It seeks to give guidance to LEAs on the means of providing 'accommodation such as takes account of the special educational needs of the pupils'* and to explain those factors relating to buildings which are taken into consideration by the Department and HMI in setting the 'recognised accommodation'† for individual schools. Most of the content therefore applies also to non-maintained special schools. The advice given should be of assistance to the providers of independent special schools and much will be of relevance to special units attached to ordinary schools. Residential accommodation is not covered in this publication.

2.2 The guidance relates to those schools most frequently provided; that is those for pupils with learning, behavioural, physical and sensory difficulties. In this publication the following acronyms are used:

EBD   emotional and behavioural difficulties
HI   hearing impairment
MLD   moderate learning difficulties
PD   physical difficulties
PMLD   profound and multiple learning difficulties
SLD   severe learning difficulties
VI   visual impairment.

Providers of schools which cover a combination of different special needs, as well as schools catering for specific learning difficulties, should interpret the information and accommodation advice as appropriate to their particular circumstances and needs. Schools for pupils with sensory difficulties are not included in the accommodation Tables 2–23, and again an assessment related to any learning and other difficulties will be necessary.

2.3 The illustrations and tables are based on what has been observed to meet curricular and other requirements in practice. The success of any special school building will depend to a considerable extent on the particular design solution, and in this respect the publication offers guidance, rather than minimum standards.

2.4 The guidance provided in this document is intended primarily to assist in the briefing and planning of new schemes but is also applicable to extensions and adaptations, both to existing special schools and to mainstream buildings being converted to special schools, as well as to the reorganisation of existing provision. Accommodation shortcomings likely to be encountered when upgrading existing special schools may include a lack of specialist teaching spaces, limited storage and, for some schools, inadequate sensory curriculum and hygiene provision. In adapting mainstream buldings there is likely to be a 'loose fit' necessitating a greater overall area than for new construction, with associated higher running costs. Often measures will be necessary to overcome problems of access and circulation as well as those of storage and, where appropriate, provision for the sensory curriculum and hygiene.

2.5 The accommodation needs referred to in Chapters 3 and 4 are reflected in the notional area schedules given in Chapter 6. These schedules are based upon a 'menu' (Table 1) which lists potential uses of teaching spaces of different sizes. The list is not comprehensive but is intended to inform the selection of room size (or the assessment of the suitability of existing rooms) for the educational needs of a potential group of pupils, related to their age and difficulties. Illustrations of how many of these spaces might be planned or used in practice are shown throughout Chapters 3 and 4, along with some examples of actual provision seen. Tables 14–16 suggest teaching area per pupil according to age, need and the size of school, and Table 23 projects this for gross area to give an indication of the likely overall building area suitable for use in the earliest feasibility stages of a scheme.

*Education (School Premises) Regulations 1981, paragraph 8(2).

†Recognised accommodation is the provision required for the number, age-range, gender and special needs of pupils for whom a school is approved by DFE, and whether such provision is day, boarding or both.

3 | Main teaching accommodation

3.1 The Education Reform Act 1988 sets out the requirements for a balanced and broadly based curriculum including the National Curriculum and religious education. These requirements should be given high priority in the planning and provision of accommodation in all maintained schools including special schools.

3.2 Pupil organisation needs to take into account the following factors so as to ensure that all pupils have access to an appropriate curriculum, including provision for their social development:

- the optimum number of pupils per class group in relation to their particular special educational needs and in relation to specialist subjects and the nature of the activity being undertaken

- class/tutorial groups, probably based on chronological age, although in small special schools two or more year groups may have to be combined

- flexibility in grouping to meet individual learning needs

- an appropriate environment, whether in separate primary and secondary special schools or in all-age special schools.

3.3 The accommodation requirements below are set out in the context of general requirements which apply to all special schools, followed by additional requirements for particular groups of pupils whose special needs require a broadly similar range of resources to support learning. These broad groupings are intended only as a guide to the nature of accommodation suitable for the pupils and will need to be modified in the light of particular local circumstances. In the case of special schools for other groups, such as pupils with speech and language difficulties or pupils with autistic behaviours, it should be possible to use the information in 'General requirements' together with relevant

Illustration 1
One-to-one tuition

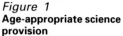

Figure 1
Age-appropriate science provision
1a. Primary science delivered in the practical area of a class base by supplementing the classroom provision with a science resource trolley from a central store, which would probably be associated with a separate, fitted practical bay available to all classes.

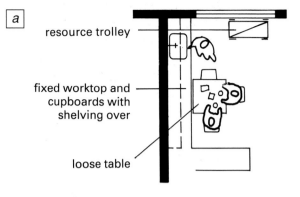

resource trolley

fixed worktop and cupboards with shelving over

loose table

1b. A specially fitted and equipped science room of 45m² for a secondary age group with preparation room and store off, furnished for a class of eight pupils with moderate learning difficulties.

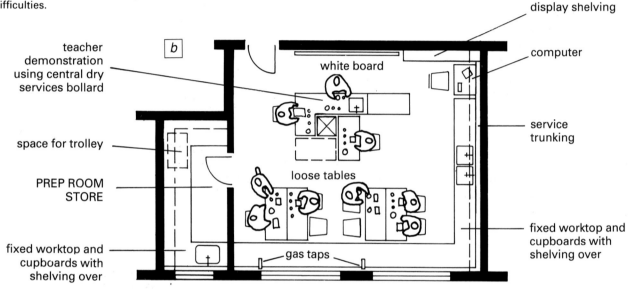

display shelving

teacher demonstration using central dry services bollard

white board

computer

space for trolley

service trunking

PREP ROOM STORE

loose tables

fixed worktop and cupboards with shelving over

fixed worktop and cupboards with shelving over

gas taps

1   0   1   2   3   4   5   6   7m

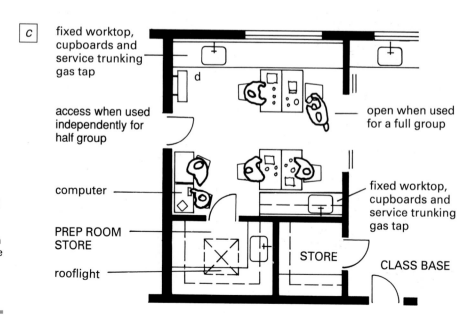

fixed worktop, cupboards and service trunking gas tap

access when used independently for half group

open when used for a full group

1c. A fitted and equipped science nucleus of 25m² plus preparation room/store located adjacent to a class base for use independently for a half group or combined with the base for a full group. Suitable either as the only dedicated science provision in a very small secondary school or as an additional science space in a larger school.

computer

PREP ROOM STORE

rooflight

fixed worktop, cupboards and service trunking gas tap

STORE

CLASS BASE

4

parts of other additional sections to assist in the planning of such specialist provision.

General requirements

All special schools

3.4   Where staffing levels are implemented in accordance with guidance in DES Circular 11/90[3], groups will generally include between six and 10 pupils. Teaching spaces need to be large enough to accommodate several adults as, in addition to teachers, there are likely to be special support assistants and possibly therapists or other specialist staff working within the class bases for some or all of the time. The accommodation should be planned for flexibility in the way it can be used so as to cater for future developments in teaching methods and changes in pupil intake.

3.5   Accommodation needs to be provided for:

- each class group to have its own class base, to give pupils a sense of stability and facilities to store their books and belongings and to meet the need for a significant pastoral relationship, although some classrooms may support subject specialisms

- some specially equipped teaching accommodation which is distinct from class bases and which includes practical areas for science, art and food and design technology, the extent of such provision depending upon the age of the pupils

- variety of sizes of teaching spaces, including small group rooms

- facilities which take account of the particular learning needs of the pupils.

3.6   Provision needs to be made for pupils to experience physical education, drama and music. In smaller schools this may be in a multi-purpose hall, but in larger schools the number of groups requiring access to such facilities means that separate areas may need to be provided (see also Chapter 4).

3.7   Suitable space, storage and display facilities need to be provided for books and other resources, both within teaching areas and also in a separate library/ resource area.

Illustration 2
Infants' class showing teacher-formed activity areas

3.8　A good supply of electrical sockets will enable the flexible use of computers and other electronic aids and equipment. It is important to ensure that there are sufficient sockets situated around the rooms so that wires are not trailing and extension leads do not have to be used.

3.9　In all-age schools positive attempts need to be made to ensure that the primary environment reflects the age of the pupils. Similarly, as pupils progress through the school those of secondary age should have access to a more adult environment which not only facilitates co-operative group work but supports individual study, investigation and research.

Accommodation needs at primary level

3.10　Nursery provision in a special school differs little from that elsewhere, but there may be fewer children and a greater number of staff for each nursery class. Additional equipment, which is often bulky, is also likely to be needed. Not all pupils will necessarily have special needs as some nurseries based in special schools operate as local neighbourhood nurseries, with pupils integrated with others from the local community. One function of the special school nursery may be to assess appropriate future placement for individual pupils with special educational needs.

3.11　Each primary class should have its own base similar to those in well-designed modern primary schools, preferably with direct access to the outside. Sufficient space is required to support the curriculum as well as to accommodate the appropriate numbers of pupils and staff. For example, the base for a group of infants should be of a size that allows for a range of activities to be pursued at any one time, including those involving imaginative and constructional play, and the use of large equipment such as a slide or wheeled toys. The teacher will also want to be able to create a quiet area to support individual or group work.

Illustration 3
Small group using shared practical bay

3.12 Although much practical work is likely to take place in class bases, some specially equipped teaching space should be provided. Hygienic conditions for food technology should be separate from provision for science and design technology. Bays which are suitable for half groups of pupils and are equipped with solid benches and with access to electricity, water and storage may be adequate. Where schools are large, practical bays can be supplemented by resource trolleys for use in class bases.

Accommodation needs at secondary level

3.13 The requirement for each class to have its own base remains, although it is likely that pupils will move around different teaching areas. Some of these may also support subject specialisms such as mathematics, humanities or modern foreign languages, with resources and materials being concentrated in particular bases.

3.14 Specially equipped teaching areas, together with associated storage and preparation areas, need to be provided for science, food technology and design technology and for work in two- and three-dimensional art. These areas should not double as class bases, a practice which both disadvantages the class concerned and limits the use which can be made of such facilities. Where space is limited in a small school this can sometimes be resolved by the use of a 'nucleus' specialist area adjacent to a class base, which may then be used either separately for a half group or in conjunction with the base for a full group.

3.15 More extensive provision for a library and other resource materials needs to be made. It will be helpful if space and facilities are included to enable pupils to undertake individual study and to use reference materials. Such an area will both support the curriculum generally and will provide space for pupils to relax and enjoy reading and browsing.

Accommodation for post-16 students

3.16 The planning of post-16 provision should be age-appropriate and it should be designed to recognise students approaching adult status. Accommodation for post-16 students should have a more adult ethos. It should include space for work in a more social setting with facilities for students to take breaks and to make drinks as well as space for more formal teaching sessions. The accommodation used as a base for post-16 students should be available for their exclusive use rather than shared with younger pupils. As the accommodation will be for students aged 16–19, it is important that there is sufficient space to allow for separate groups pursuing different activities to operate within the accommodation.

Illustration 4
Library

3.17   In some LEAs the pattern of provision for 16–19 will be based on schools, either for policy reasons or for reasons associated with the geographical difficulty of making more central post-16 provision. Where this is the case, provision should be made for students at special schools to continue in post-16 education. Because of the need to recognise adult status, post-16 provision should be distinct from the school provision and preferably in separate accommodation within the building, although using some of the specialist facilities.

3.18   Where provision is school-based, courses for post-16 students should include some teaching within the school together with the opportunity to have experience of learning in a more adult setting, such as attending courses at a further education college and undertaking work experience, with suitable areas for the discussion and reinforcement of these experiences and for writing up and displaying work which arises from them. Small spaces for discussion with tutors and individual counselling should be provided. For students for whom the further development of social and independence skills is necessary, the accommodation should include appropriately sized independent living areas,

where such skills can be practised and developed in an adult setting. Some special schools have arranged for this by means of access to a house or flat in the locality, rather than by accommodation on site.

3.19   In other LEAs there is a policy of placing post-16 provision in further education colleges, tertiary colleges or sixth form colleges, rather than in secondary schools. Within such a setting there should be opportunities for students with physical and/or learning difficulties to have access to appropriate courses. This may involve a range of courses including some discrete courses, arrangements for support within mainstream courses and also opportunities to participate in vocational courses, Certificate of Pre-Vocational Education courses and work experience. It is important in order to allow students with special educational needs to develop their full potential that they should be recognised as part of the student body and have access to general post-16 facilities rather than being provided for as a separate group. The accommodation and staffing of colleges or centres should be planned to take account of the particular needs of these students so that there is appropriate provision for physical access, for

Figure 2
Life skills unit
A small flat adjacent to main teaching base for post-16 pupils. The living room might be used as a social area, with table tennis table, etc from store. Where some pupils are in wheelchairs, the bathroom and kitchen need to provide for suitable working heights and suitable access to permit independent living skills practice.

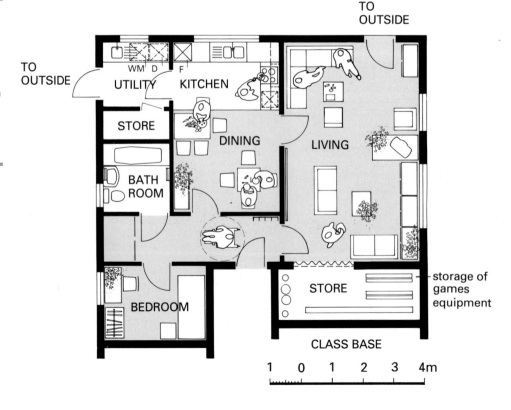

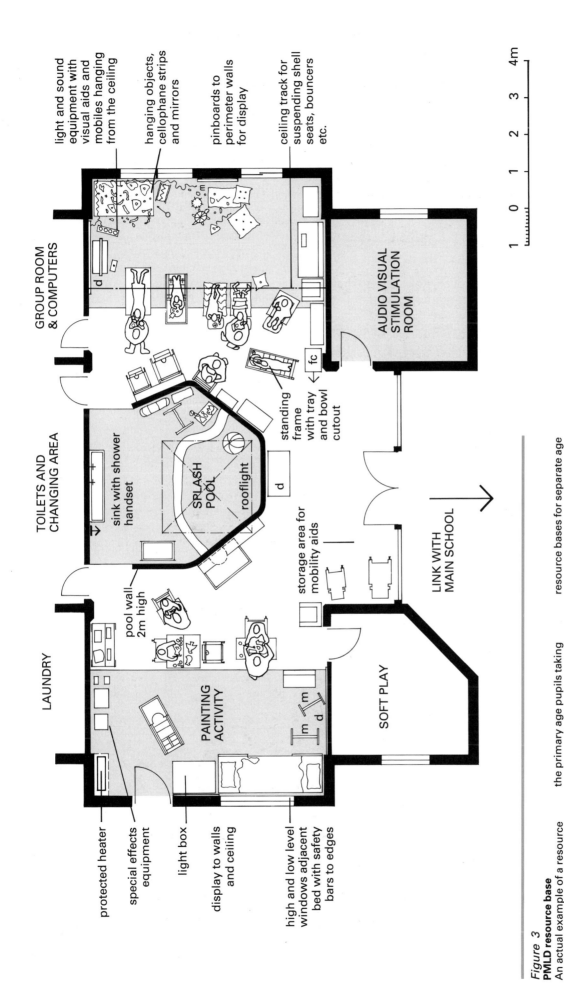

light and sound equipment with visual aids and mobiles hanging from the ceiling

hanging objects, cellophane strips and mirrors

pinboards to perimeter walls for display

ceiling track for suspending shell seats, bouncers etc.

GROUP ROOM & COMPUTERS

TOILETS AND CHANGING AREA

LAUNDRY

AUDIO VISUAL STIMULATION ROOM

sink with shower handset

SPLASH POOL

rooflight

standing frame with tray and bowl cutout

fc

pool wall 2m high

d

LINK WITH MAIN SCHOOL

storage area for mobility aids

protected heater

special effects equipment

light box

display to walls and ceiling

high and low level windows adjacent bed with safety bars to edges

PAINTING ACTIVITY

SOFT PLAY

m m

d

1 0 1 2 3 4m

Figure 3
PMLD resource base
An actual example of a resource base for pupils with profound and multiple learning difficulties attached to an all-age SLD school. The base is divided into separate areas for primary and secondary age pupils with adjacent pool, sensory curriculum and hygiene areas. The afternoon session illustrated shows the primary age pupils taking part in sand and water activities. The secondary age pupils are painting. In practice it has been found that the storage space for mobility aids is too small and that the entrance to the audio-visual room is restricted, especially for pupils in wheelchairs. For a new scheme resource bases for separate age groups, each located within the primary or secondary area of the school, and taking into account the practical difficulties noted above, would be appropriate.

suitable acoustic conditions in lecture rooms and other areas, and for toilets and privacy for self care along the lines of, but in simpler form than, that suggested for special schools in Chapters 3 and 4.

Additional requirements for special schools catering for particular groups of pupils

Schools for pupils with severe learning difficulties

3.20   Pupils with severe learning difficulties demonstrate a range of abilities with about one-third having profound and multiple learning difficulties. Pupils may also have some degree of sensory or physical impairment; a few may have disturbed behaviour. Current trends suggest that the proportion of pupils with multiple difficulties is increasing.

Educational needs

3.21   Grouping pupils in the school according to chronological age is more likely to ensure access to an appropriate curriculum and has the advantages of helping teachers to create an age-appropriate learning environment and allowing pupils the experience of progressing through a series of classes as do their peers in ordinary schools. Where this is possible, there are implications for space and storage requirements as in all class bases some pupils may need to use a wide range of aids and equipment including wheelchairs and other specialist seating, standing frames and prone boards. Suitable toilet and changing areas need to be located throughout the school.

3.22   Where chronological grouping of pupils is not feasible, for example in small special schools, particular care is needed to ensure that pupils have access

Illustration 5
Special support assistant with PMLD pupil

to a curriculum, to learning materials and to resources and equipment which are appropriate for their particular age.

3.23   The range of learning needs likely to be found in any one class can be met by flexibly grouping pupils according to ability within and across classes. Such groupings may be necessary in core subject work.

3.24   Where segregated grouping on the basis of disability is retained, design should facilitate increasing integration, so that such pupils can take part in learning and social activities with their peers rather than always being part of a separate group with a wide age range.

3.25   As these pupils require frequent support from teachers and special support assistants, the adult:pupil ratio will be high and this needs to be taken into account in determining the size of the teaching areas. They may need access to other specialist staff, for example teachers of pupils with hearing or visual impairment, physiotherapists, speech therapists or occupational therapists. These additional needs of pupils with profound and multiple learning difficulties can be supported by a resource base which pupils can use for individual or small group activity with specialist teachers and assistants.

3.26   Specialist equipment, aids and curriculum materials to support learning are necessary. In bases where there are pupils with profound and multiple learning difficulties there should be some glazing down to floor level to enable those who are at floor level to see out beyond their immediate surroundings and preferably have sight of some activity or interesting and attractive view. However, provision should still be made for means to position pupils at a variety of levels. Ceiling displays are important and provision must be made for the suspension of possibly heavy weights, including slings and hammocks. Adequate storage facilities adjacent to classrooms facilitate ease of access to equipment and materials, and prevent clutter and encroachment on space for teaching and learning.

3.27   There is likely to be regular consultation between school staff and families of pupils, and with staff from other community and voluntary agencies, so suitable private accommodation for discussion and meetings needs to be provided.

Accommodation needs at primary level

3.28   Some pupils with severe learning difficulties are equipped with large amounts of mobile/semi-mobile infor-

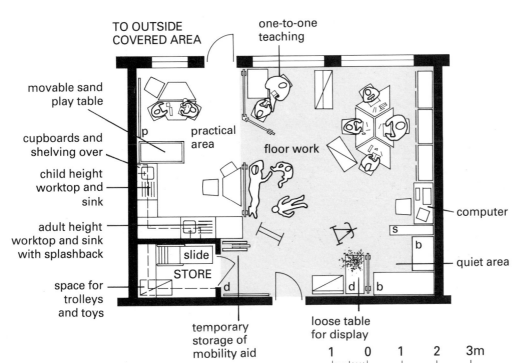

TO OUTSIDE COVERED AREA

one-to-one teaching

movable sand play table

practical area

floor work

cupboards and shelving over

child height worktop and sink

adult height worktop and sink with splashback

space for trolleys and toys

slide

STORE

computer

quiet area

temporary storage of mobility aid

loose table for display

1   0   1   2   3m

Figure 4
Primary SLD class base
A class base of 54m² suitable for eight pupils with severe learning difficulties shown engaged in various activities. Some are doing table work with the teacher or independently in the practical area; others are involved in floor work with a special support assistant and one is receiving individual attention from a visiting therapist. The room has been arranged to include a computer space and a quiet corner. The unfurnished central space will at other times be used for play or work involving equipment from the store.

mation technology and audio-visual equipment which present demands on space and accommodation.

3.29   Facilities to support the sensory curriculum, which is an essential part of many pupils' development, include light/sound stimulation, soft play (including ball pools), and warm water pools (see also Chapter 4). Warm water provides a most effective medium for muscle relaxation and exercising.

Accommodation needs at secondary level

3.30   Each class needs its own base. The base for school leavers should promote and reflect their independence and post-school aspirations. It should contain facilities for individual and group work, for leisure activities and for making drinks and simple snacks.

3.31   Separate specialist teaching facilities for science, design technology and food technology are required. A suite of rooms, including living and dining areas, bedroom, bathroom, lavatory and kitchen, should be provided which allows students to implement the inde-

pendence skills necessary for community living.

Schools for pupils with moderate learning difficulties

3.32   Schools for pupils with moderate learning difficulties can expect to accommodate pupils with a range of learning difficulties. The ability range is likely to overlap both with pupils found in ordinary schools and with pupils in schools for severe learning difficulties, but will depend on particular local circumstances. The accommodation requirements are likely to be similar to those for ordinary schools, except for class sizes and the implications of a higher staff: pupil ratio. It may therefore be easier to adapt redundant ordinary school buildings for use as special schools for pupils with moderate learning difficulties than for other special needs. There is usually not the same need for extensive paramedical, hygiene and therapy provision as is the case in schools for pupils with severe learning difficulties. However, some is necessary, and the extent is dependent upon the types and degrees of pupils' difficulties.

Figure 5
Secondary PMLD base
A resource base of 72m² for eight pupils with profound and multiple learning difficulties with bulk store and WC/hygiene area opening off. Furniture divides the room into more intimate areas, suitable for withdrawal from participation in activities elsewhere in the school, including a quiet one-to-one corner, an uncarpeted practical area, a rest or exercise corner with foam mats and a central informal space for small groups.

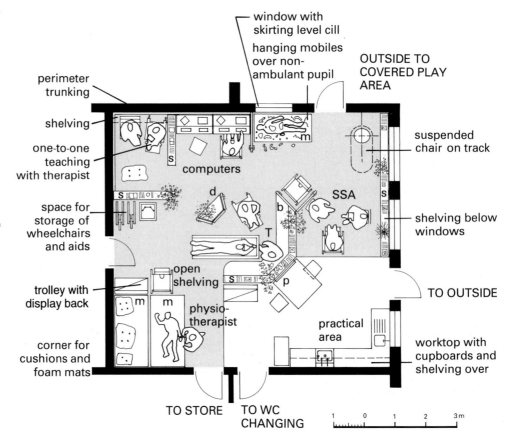

Illustration 6
Social/dining space in life skills area

Illustration 7
Specialist food technology area

Educational needs

3.33 Schools for pupils with moderate learning difficulties need the capacity to organise the teaching and learning so that flexible grouping can take place. Within the overall teacher:pupil ratio pupils may be organised for some activities into larger or smaller groups. Such schools are frequently expected to make provision both for younger pupils identified as having very complex needs and older pupils who transfer from secondary schools. Schools need to be organised so as to be able to respond to unpredictable admission demands; these often arise from the changing ability of ordinary schools to meet the needs of pupils with special educational needs. Thus close working relationships with ordinary schools and regular liaison about potential admissions are needed as well as accommodation suitable for such liaison meetings.

Accommodation needs at primary level

3.34 For the early years, pupils need sufficient space for structured play, small group table work and quiet one-to-one work.

3.35 For pupils of primary age, class bases, linked where possible with shared practical areas and with access to science and technology bays, are needed. It may be advantageous to enable teachers to plan together so that two or three class bases can share facilities. Where possible class bases should have quiet areas for listening, reading and writing and other space, perhaps shared, in an adjoining area for practical and investigational work.

Accommodation needs at secondary level

3.36 For pupils of secondary age, class bases are still needed but movement to other specialist areas can be expected. Some class bases may also serve as resource bases for particular aspects of the curriculum such as humanities, mathematics, modern foreign languages or work associated with modular

Figure 6
Primary MLD class base
A class base of 45m² for a group of 10 pupils with moderate learning difficulties shown pursuing alternative class activities. In 6a they are all engaged on tablework with assistance from the teacher and a special support assistant, while in 6b most are involved in 'making and doing' centred around the practical area. At other times the tables would be stacked away to create space for constructive play. An alternative arrangement would be for the room to link with other class bases and shared practical space, perhaps serving as a particular resource base, for example for mathematics.

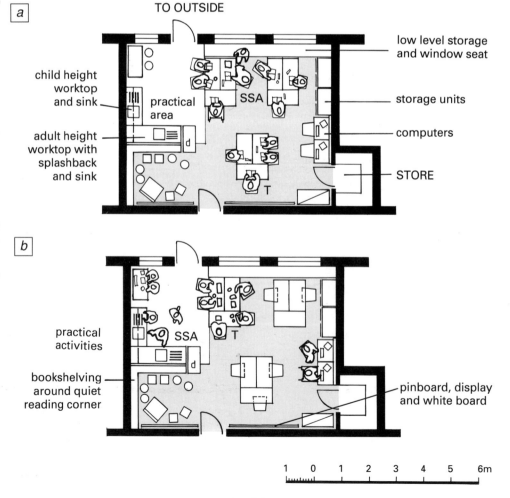

courses. Specially equipped areas for science, food, design technology and art need to be so positioned as to facilitate work across these areas of the curriculum.

3.37   For pupils in the final two years of schooling, accommodation should include both teaching space and an informal area with a more adult ethos to assist in the preparation of such pupils for college-based courses or work.

3.38   Accommodation should have a distinctively secondary flavour with space available for small group discussion, independent learning supporting practical and investigational activities, and listening and writing activities making use of audio equipment and word processors. Provision should be made for individual study. The accommodation should also foster opportunities for structured informal dialogues about pupil progress associated with Records of Achievement. Provision for pupils in Years 10 and 11 should include facilities relating to careers work and links with further education and industry. An appropriate social facility is also desir-

able for these older pupils, perhaps associated with a leavers' base.

Schools catering for pupils with moderate and with severe learning difficulties

3.39   There will be a wider range of learning difficulties in such schools than in separate schools for pupils with moderate learning difficulties and those with severe learning difficulties. The same principles of curriculum entitlement apply. Class/tutorial groups based on chronological age with flexibility of grouping to meet individual learning needs will encourage cohesion.

Schools for pupils with emotional and behavioural difficulties

3.40   Pupils placed in special schools on account of their emotional and behavioural difficulties span a wide range of ability. Many, though not all, may have significant learning difficulties as a result of their emotional and behavioural problems, and are less likely to

Figure 7
Secondary MLD/PD linked subject bases
An actual example of adjacent linked class bases in a school for pupils with moderate learning difficulties, including pupils with physical difficulties. One base has developed an English specialism, the other mathematics. The shared room between the bases was intended to be a quiet, small group room but staff have chosen to use it for computer work. The arrangement permits the teachers to work flexibly and co-operatively, making efficient use of the shared resources.

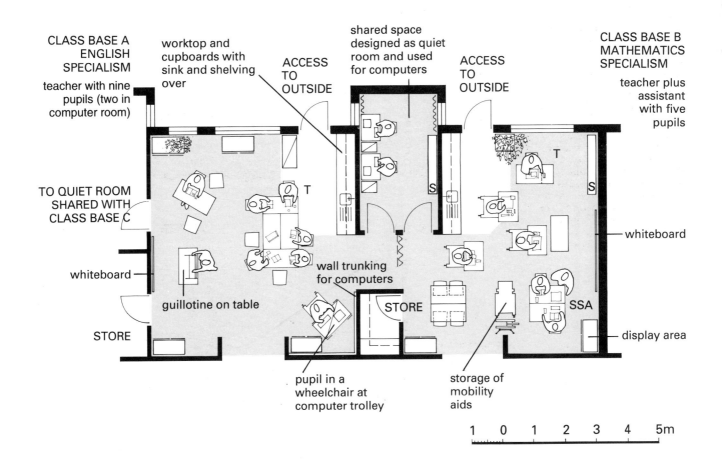

Figure 8
Design technology provision

8a. Specialist teaching area of a secondary or all-age school with linked practical spaces for design technology and two- and three-dimensional art plus shared computer/resource room. Separate science and food technology rooms are adjacent. The provision shown would serve a school for about 80–120 secondary age pupils, with some design work probably taking place in the class bases. By adding a second science room and another design technology space, with a clean design area, the provision would be appropriate for a larger school.

8b. A design technology area of 85m² providing a multi-materials workshop and a separate design space. The teacher has organised a lesson whereby the technician is supervising some work in the practical area while other pupils work on design and planning activities with the teacher.

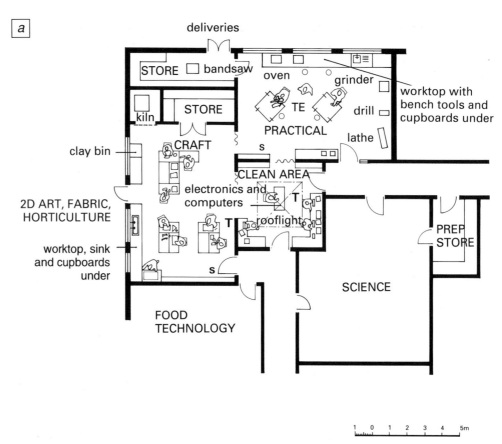

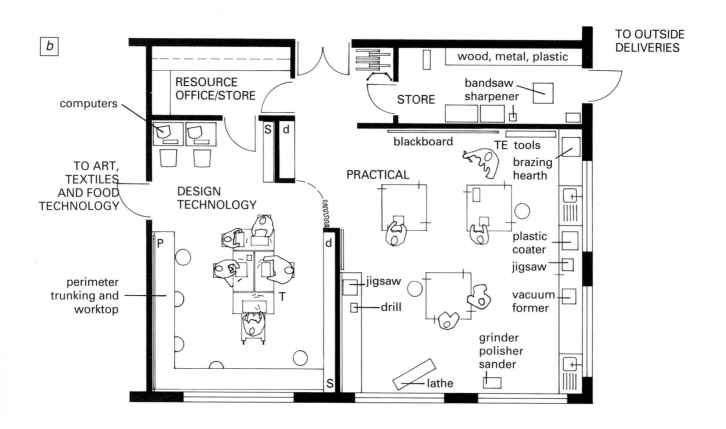

16

become spontaneously involved in learning activities. Their attitudes towards and capacities for learning will vary considerably.

3.41 Special schools for pupils with emotional and behavioural difficulties tend to be small. Although they vary in size, most such schools cater for between 45 and 65 pupils. Generally there is a much higher proportion of boys than girls than is the case in other types of special school.

Educational needs

3.42 Class bases generally need to be large enough for groups of up to eight pupils as well as, in many instances, more than one adult. Separate provision for case conferences, interviews, meetings and support of parents and carers will ensure a greater degree of privacy. An essential consideration is that pupils should be able to work at sufficient distance from each other so as to minimise disturbances and distractions,

including interference by other pupils. Periods of withdrawal from the group may be needed. These schools are therefore relatively demanding of space. In addition to greater space standards there is a need for a robust and resilient environment which should nevertheless provide attractive surroundings.

Accommodation needs at primary level

3.43 For pupils of primary age there needs to be sufficient space for work with both small and large equipment, areas for messy activities and a comfortable and attractive book and listening corner. Supervision is especially important, and for this reason regularly shaped rooms without hidden corners are preferable.

Accommodation needs at secondary level

3.44 Older pupils need access to classroom/study bases which reflect their

Illustration 8
Art and craft area

move towards adulthood. Within these areas it should be possible to have individual work spaces and an area which supports informal group discussion, careers guidance and aspects of the curriculum which deserve a more flexible approach. An area that can be designated for leisure and social purposes, perhaps linked with a leavers' base, is also of value.

Schools for pupils with physical difficulties

3.45 Pupils with physical difficulties may also have sensory, speech or learning difficulties, presenting a range of complex educational needs. Mobility problems will range from slight to severe involving full-time use of a wheelchair. The degree or nature of the physical disability is not necessarily a pointer to the range of educational difficulties which may be experienced.

Educational needs

3.46 The educational needs of many pupils can be met effectively only where

treatment, support and advice are available from medical, nursing and paramedical staff, including physiotherapists, occupational therapists and speech and language therapists. Although the provision of separate treatment rooms is necessary, much of the work of therapists takes place in the classrooms. Many pupils depend on a wide variety of aids and equipment to assist their education, mobility, seating, communication, personal care and daily living. These require space and often access to electrical sockets. A single child may use three different wheelchairs: one in which to reach the school, one to move around the building and another within teaching spaces. This has implications for storage areas (see Chapter 4).

3.47 Access to the whole curriculum involves access not only to rooms but also to work surfaces and practical areas in order that each pupil can work as independently as possible, as and when appropriate.

3.48 Educational needs are best met in groups of six to eight pupils, with a

Figure 9
Primary EBD class bases
An actual example of two infant class bases for pupils with emotional and behavioural difficulties in a building designed as an ordinary primary school. Each room is arranged in a way which provides areas for different activities. This has been achieved by the teachers using furniture to screen or segregate spaces for play, for quiet work or for one-to-one teaching. The class base sizes of about 45m² (small for a mainstream school) are suitable for the high staff: pupil ratio and for the 'personal space' needed.

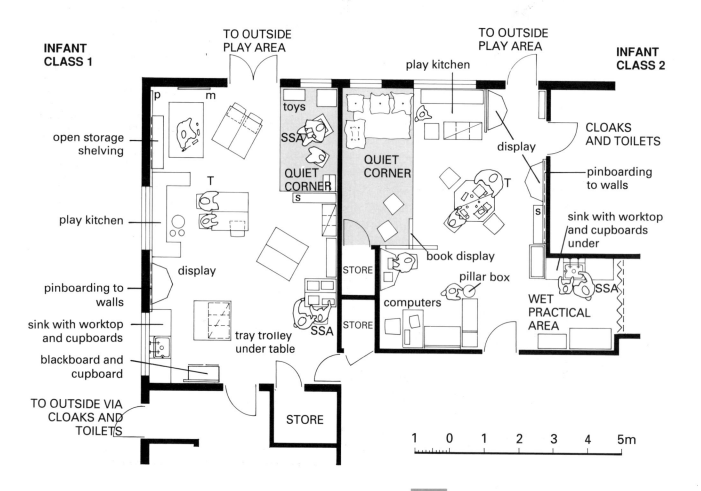

Illustration 9
Use of computers

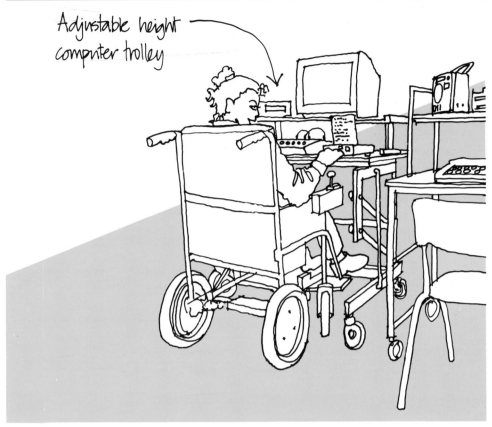

Adjustable height computer trolley

Figure 10
Secondary EBD classbase
A class base of 36m² for, at most, eight secondary age pupils with emotional and behavioural difficulties who will spend a significant amount of time in specialist teaching areas elsewhere in the school. There should be sufficient space for each pupil to have an individual desk or table, as in 10a. It will also be possible for tables to be clustered for group work, as in 10b where, for example, four pupils are working together with a teacher. Sufficient space is also available for other pupils to be engaged in practical work, individual study and working alongside other adults.

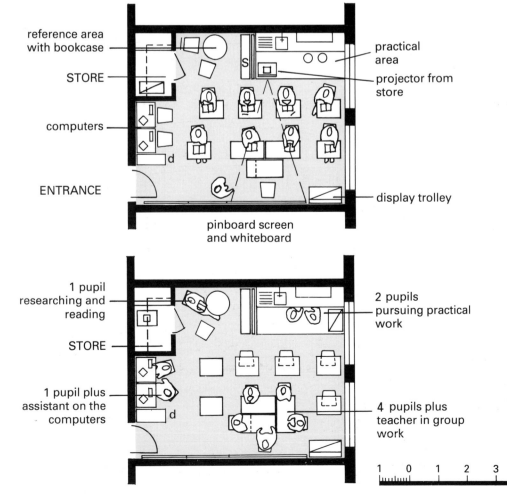

reference area with bookcase

STORE

computers

ENTRANCE

practical area

projector from store

display trolley

pinboard screen and whiteboard

1 pupil researching and reading

STORE

1 pupil plus assistant on the computers

2 pupils pursuing practical work

4 pupils plus teacher in group work

1 0 1 2 3 4 5 6m

teacher and one or more special support assistants to each group. Space should be adequate to enable intensive work with one or two pupils to take place either within the classroom or nearby.

3.49 Conductive education and programmes based on the principles of Peto are being increasingly included in the curriculum, particularly for younger children. Where this is the case, allowance needs to be made for space both for the use of the equipment and for storage when it is not in use, as well as for additional adults.

Accommodation needs at primary level

3.50 Classrooms need to be large enough for pupils' independent and assisted movement and to accommodate a wide range of equipment and aids, including wheelchairs, mobility and posture aids, specialist furniture, etc, both while in use and while temporarily unused.

3.51 Space is particularly important where the plinths, chairs and stools used in conductive education need to be moved regularly during the day. Temporary storage for educational materials and equipment should not create hazards at floor level.

3.52 Many of the pupils use electronic aids to learning which require safe and convenient access to electrical services.

3.53 A considerable number of pupils have problems of incontinence. Hygiene and toilet areas should be large enough to provide access for wheelchairs and to enable several adults to help safely with any lifting, and provide suitably sized changing tables for pupils requiring total assistance. Privacy should be ensured for all parts of the facility (see also Chapter 4).

Illustration 10
Conductive education class

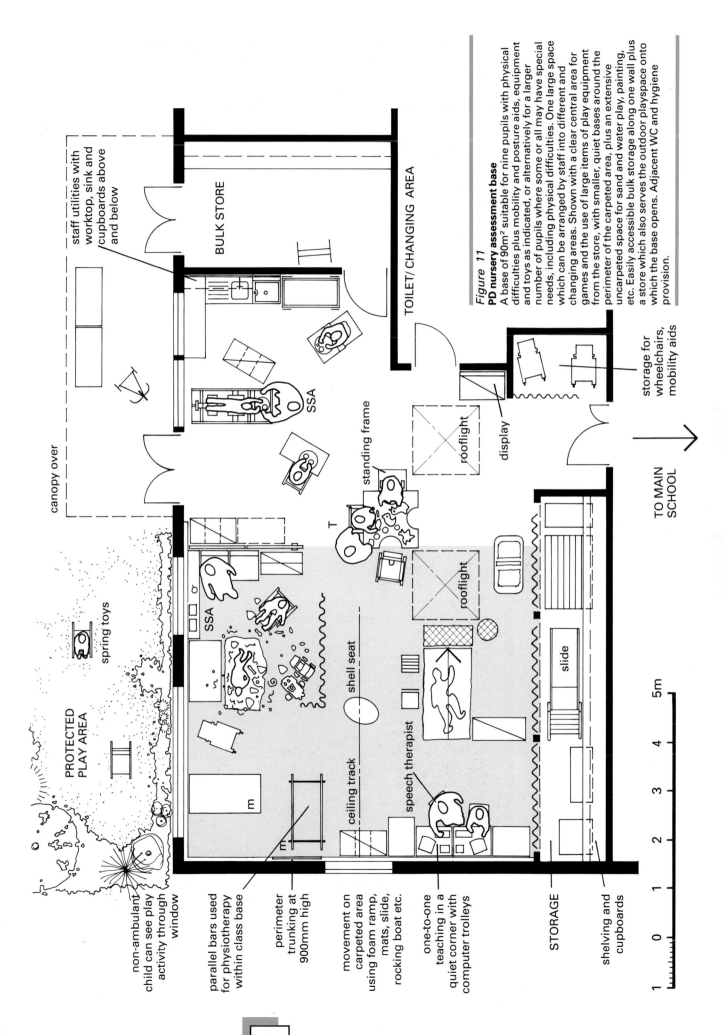

staff utilities with worktop, sink and cupboards above and below

BULK STORE

canopy over

TOILET/ CHANGING AREA

SSA

SSA

standing frame

storage for wheelchairs, mobility aids

rooflight

display

T

rooflight

TO MAIN SCHOOL

spring toys

non-ambulant child can see play activity through window

PROTECTED PLAY AREA

m

shell seat

ceiling track

speech therapist

slide

STORAGE

m

m

parallel bars used for physiotherapy within class base

perimeter trunking at 900mm high

movement on carpeted area using foam ramp, mats, slide, rocking boat etc.

one-to-one teaching in a quiet corner with computer trolleys

shelving and cupboards

0   1   2   3   4   5m

Figure 11

PD nursery assessment base

A base of 90m² suitable for nine pupils with physical difficulties plus mobility and posture aids, equipment and toys as indicated, or alternatively for a larger number of pupils where some or all may have special needs, including physical difficulties. One large space which can be arranged by staff into different and changing areas. Shown with a clear central area for games and the use of large items of play equipment from the store, with smaller, quiet bases around the perimeter of the carpeted area, plus an extensive uncarpeted space for sand and water play, painting, etc. Easily accessible bulk storage along one wall plus a store which also serves the outdoor playspace onto which the base opens. Adjacent WC and hygiene provision.

Accommodation needs at secondary level

3.54 Secondary classrooms need to allow for the larger special furniture and equipment used by these pupils.

3.55 Specially equipped teaching areas are necessary for two- and three-dimensional art, design technology, science and cooking, covering both food technology and social/life skills. Kitchen bays should include different worktop heights providing for both the ambulant and non-ambulant. Such areas need equipment or aids appropriate to the physical and learning difficulties of the pupils for independent learning. In these areas teaching may be in smaller groups.

Schools for pupils with visual impairment

3.56 Pupils with visual disability are relatively few in number and they span the full breadth of intellectual ability. Special schools increasingly cater for the entire range of visual impairment from total blindness to useful but impaired vision, although there still remains differentiation between establishments that meet the needs of those who require tactile or visual methods of working. The population in special schools has been affected by the increasingly successful integration of pupils with visual impairment into ordinary schools, and a greater proportion of pupils with visual impairment still in special schools have additional difficulties, such as physical, learning or behavioural.

Educational needs

3.57 The principal need of pupils with visual impairment is for access to the whole curriculum, and they use a range of special aids and equipment, such as raised surface desks or desk stands and suitably adapted teaching materials.

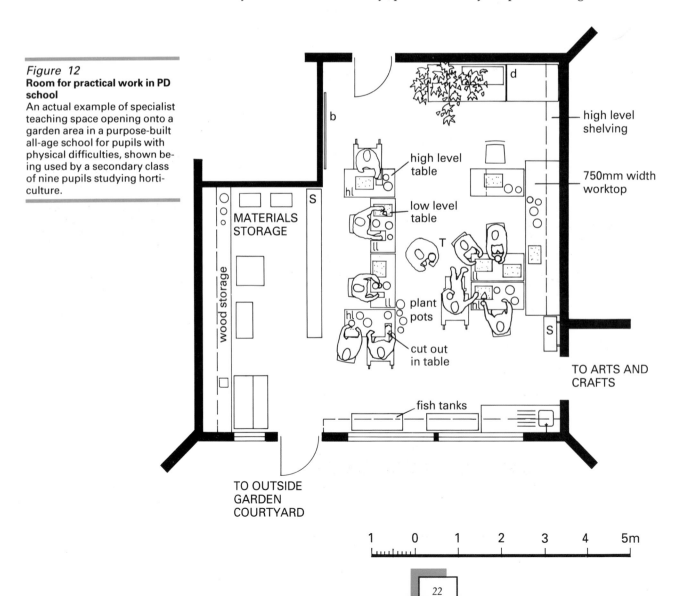

Figure 12
Room for practical work in PD school
An actual example of specialist teaching space opening onto a garden area in a purpose-built all-age school for pupils with physical difficulties, shown being used by a secondary class of nine pupils studying horticulture.

They are often taught in groups of six to eight pupils, with a teacher and one or two special support assistants to each group. Pupils may also receive specialist teaching in braille, and mobility and social skill training. This may take place in class, in specially equipped rooms, or around the school and in the local environment. Some pupils may be able to achieve the highest levels of the National Curriculum, and the accommodation and equipment should be able to support the specialist and practical work required. Other pupils require accommodation and resources more suited to pupils with severe learning difficulties.

3.58   Specific guidance on lighting and acoustic criteria for these schools, and general advice on the design of spaces for these pupils, are given in *Design Note 25: Lighting and acoustic criteria for the visually handicapped and hearing impaired in schools*[4], which should be read in conjunction with this document. Good, well-controlled natural and artificial lighting, with the elimination of glare, is required in all teaching spaces. Some visually impaired pupils may need areas with lower illumination levels, some may need task lighting, particularly for practical work. Good acoustic conditions are necessary. Special conditions exist concerning safety, and careful consideration should be given to appropriate warning and alarm systems, and to means of escape.

3.59   Because the primary disability of vision may not be the only reason for which special education provision is necessary, the buildings may need to take into account the range of problems associated with physical and learning difficulties, in particular with regard to personal hygiene.

Accommodation needs at primary level

3.60   Pupils use information technology that requires access to electrical outlets and horizontal working surfaces. There should be space for the storage of braille and audio material. Small group rooms for one or two pupils and an adult working on intensive one-to-one programmes are needed to supplement classrooms, as well as the spaces needed for the specialist workers.

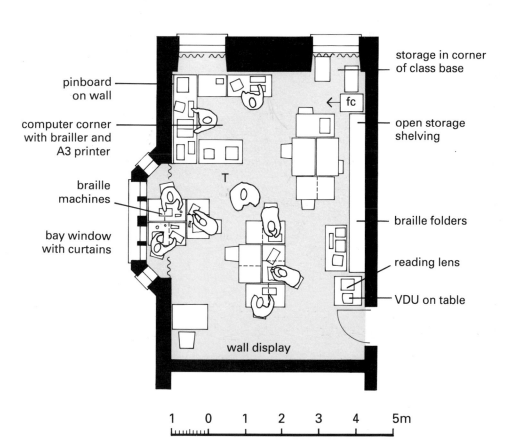

pinboard on wall

computer corner with brailler and A3 printer

braille machines

bay window with curtains

storage in corner of class base

fc

open storage shelving

braille folders

reading lens

VDU on table

wall display

Figure 13
Secondary VI class base
An actual example of a secondary class base in a converted building for pupils with visual impairment but no other significant difficulties. The base has developed an English specialism. Six pupils are engaged in a lesson with the teacher while two work independently in the computer area. There is extensive open storage along one wall.

1 0 1 2 3 4 5m

Accommodation needs at secondary level

3.61 Secondary class bases may be characterised by the concentration of equipment, books, materials and display associated with subject specialisation. They need to be large enough, and to have adequate storage space and work and display surfaces for this bulky material and the practical activities necessary to deliver the National Curriculum. Small spaces for individualised work and specialised teaching are also required. Specially equipped teaching areas require equipment appropriate to the pupils' levels of visual impairment. Consideration needs to be given to the implications on accommodation for pupils' independence training.

Additional accommodation

3.62 School libraries and resource centres need to be of sufficient size to store, besides the normal range of books, braille and large print books, audio-visual, tactile and other adapted learning resources, and the bulky hardware required to support independent research. There need to be additional rooms for the production of braille and adapted teaching materials, and the storage and repair of equipment. Rooms should also be available for medical and ophthalmic examination. Specialist workers such as mobility teachers require a base in the school.

Schools for pupils with hearing impairment

3.63 Pupils with hearing impairment in special schools may have additional difficulties such as physical, learning or behavioural difficulty. The need to concentrate specialist provision and teaching expertise means that schools for the hearing impaired are catering for a wide range of ability including very able pupils.

Illustration 11
Resources area in VI school

braille printer and book binding equipment.
laminating machine
photocopier adapted for VI.

Educational needs

3.64   Within the class bases these pupils use a range of specialist aids and equipment. Optimum group size is six to eight pupils, with a teacher and one or two special support assistants to each group. Specialists in speech, communication work and language training may work within classes or in specially equipped rooms.

3.65   Particular requirements exist for some aspects of the work, such as audiometry. Good acoustic conditions are necessary throughout the building, including larger open spaces such as halls and dining areas, and also corridors. Provision for modelling of the light to produce areas free from shadow facilitates the teaching and practising of lip-reading. Care must be taken in specifying, for example, fluorescent light fittings as some may affect certain hearing aids. Special safety conditions are required, and careful consideration should be given to appropriate visual and aural warning systems and to means of escape in an emergency.

Accommodation needs at primary level

3.66   The use of modern aids allows pupils to move more freely around the room and remain in touch with the teacher. Small group rooms for one or two pupils and an adult are needed to supplement the classroom work as well as the spaces for specialist workers.

Accommodation needs at secondary level

3.67   Class bases may develop subject specialisms to enable books, materials, display, etc to be concentrated. Nevertheless, groups are likely to remain together for many activities. Class bases should be large enough for practical work in the National Curriculum,

Illustration 12
Radio microphones in use

including space for any aids that pupils will need. Small spaces for one-to-one work are also required. As at primary level, spaces are needed to support therapists and other specialists.

3.68 Specially equipped areas need equipment appropriate to the level of hearing impairment of the pupils.

Additional accommodation

3.69 The concentration of specialist skills in schools for the hearing impaired means that such schools can make an effective contribution to supporting the needs of other pupils integrated into ordinary schools. This may take the form of work bases for peripatetic teachers and specialists; for in-house work on the preparation of teaching materials; as a source of reference material for teachers and pupils; and for in-service teacher training. If schools are also to act as such resource centres, all these functions require additional space without which this work cannot be effectively supported.

Figure 14
Primary HI class base
An infants' class base for a group of seven pupils with hearing impairment. The class is engaged on tablework and work with a computer. The room has two-directional natural lighting with blinds at all windows. Opening off the base is a one-to-one room fitted with a mirror and lighting suitable for the teaching of lip-reading.

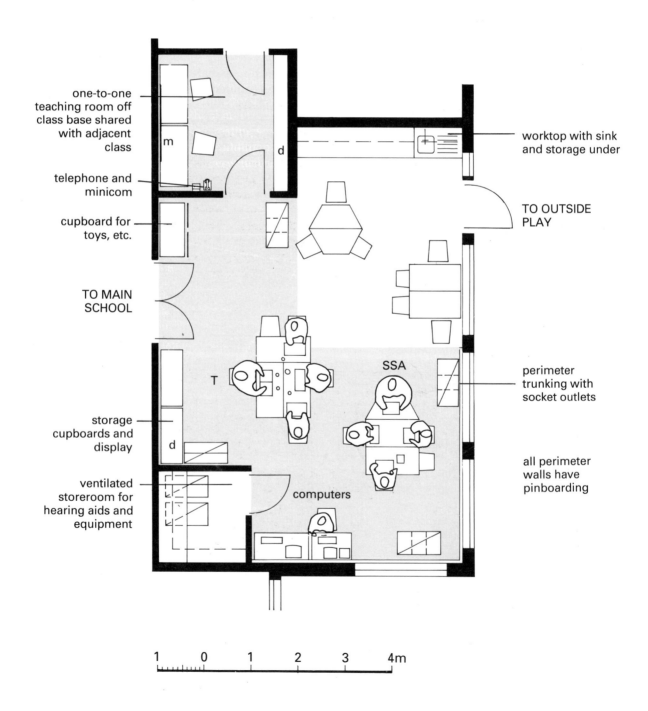

one-to-one teaching room off class base shared with adjacent class

telephone and minicom

cupboard for toys, etc.

TO MAIN SCHOOL

storage cupboards and display

ventilated storeroom for hearing aids and equipment

worktop with sink and storage under

TO OUTSIDE PLAY

perimeter trunking with socket outlets

all perimeter walls have pinboarding

SSA

computers

1 0 1 2 3 4m

4 Other accommodation

4.1 Meeting the educational needs of many pupils in special schools can require additional teaching and support provision and may place particular demands on other areas of the building, both teaching and non-teaching. Aspects of the role of special schools which may involve specific or modified accommodation can include:

- the need for support from therapists, advisory teachers, medical personnel and other specialists

- increased parental involvement

- case conferences and discussions involving staff, specialists and parents

- extensive hygiene and toilet facilities for some pupils

- greater demands on bulk storage for the large quantities of aids and equipment which may be needed

- circulation planning and design which facilitates ease of movement around the building while avoiding causing distractions or upsets for other pupils.

Generally the non-teaching area of special schools represents a significantly greater proportion of the overall area than in most ordinary schools. It is likely to be between 45% and 55% depending on the needs for which it provides (see Chapter 6).

The following sections deal with both teaching and non-teaching areas which require particular consideration.

Halls

General considerations

4.2 Because of the relatively small number of pupils in most special schools, economic considerations often dictate that a single large space must accommodate a wide variety of activities, including physical education, music, drama, dining, assemblies and collective worship, as well as open-days, school concerts, etc. In many schools the length of the working day may be

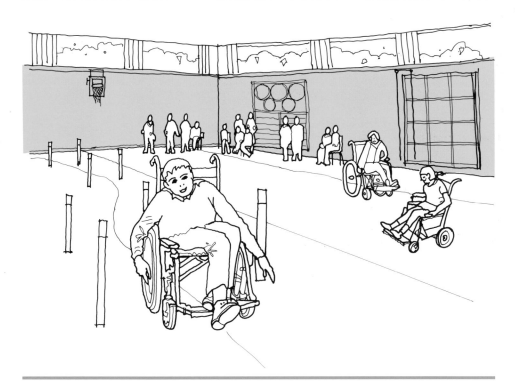

Illustration 13
Wheelchair slalom in hall

Figure 15
Hall
A hall of 120m² suitable for a small school.

15a. In use for a physical education lesson, with a group of pupils doing educational gymnastics. Equipment has been brought out of the physical education store and demountable stage units have been put away.

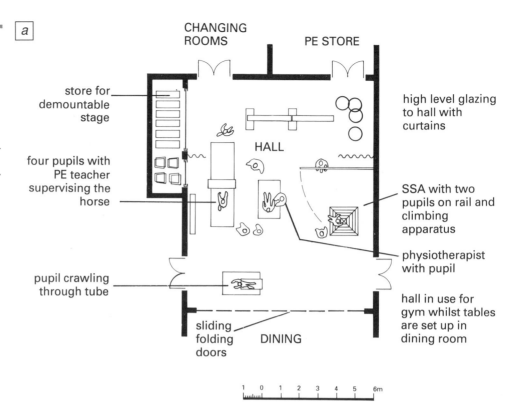

15b. The hall in use for a concert, with the stage set up and the area extended into an adjacent dining space.

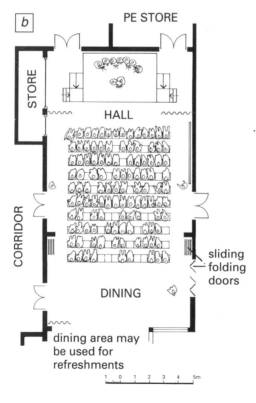

reduced by the need to allow for travelling time, for getting into and out of vehicles, and for the hygiene routines often involved at either end of the school day. Lunchtime often extends longer for pupils with special needs, for whom dining can be a learning process in itself, and when it takes place in the hall this, along with the time needed for setting out and removing the dining furniture, can conflict with the time needed for lessons. With each group of pupils requiring an appropriate number of sessions in physical education and music in a week the restrictions imposed by a single, multi-purpose space can be considerable. This often means that demands for the use of a hall are significantly greater in a special school than would be the case in an ordinary school.

4.3   Any design brief should take account of the amount of time needed in the hall for curricular and other activities. Wherever possible dining should take place in a separate area. Such an arrangement can allow a more friendly environment for dining than is possible in a multi-purpose hall. If the two spaces are adjacent they may then be combined on special occasions.

Physical education

4.4 Pupils at all types of special school need access to a large space for physical education. A hall or gymnasium will be used for floor exercises, mobility training and games, and should include an appropriate range of fixed equipment, such as wall bars, climbing frame and ropes. If possible, for secondary aged pupils these should provide sufficient space for courts for games such as badminton or basketball. Conversion of mainstream school premises for special school use is likely to include such provision, but for the number of pupils usually involved it is unlikely to be viable in other circumstances. Timetabled access to local mainstream or community facilities or alternatively a playbarn in the grounds (see Chapter 5) may provide an answer. Surfaces should not be too hard, or too noisy, especially where there are pupils with sensory impairment. Adjacent changing areas should be provided, together with space for extensive bulk storage.

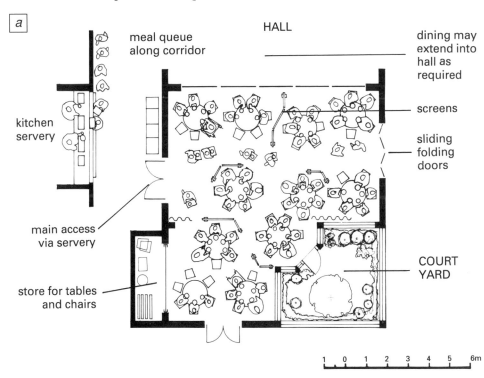

Figure 16
Dining area
A space for separate dining next to the hall illustrated in Figure 15.

16a. Lunchtime with pupils and staff in domestic scale groups. The space is divided into several areas by means of movable screens. If more pupils were in wheelchairs the arrangement of furniture would need to provide more space for access than that shown.

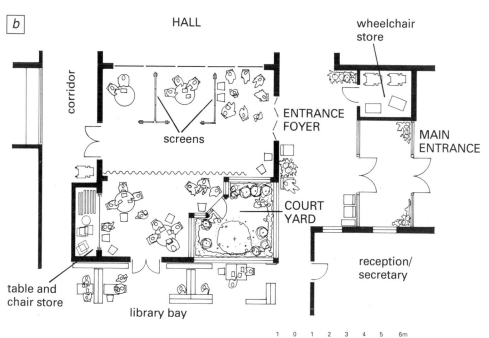

16b. The same space at other times of the day used as an extension of the adjacent library bay and for small tutorial groups. The hall and/or dining areas may also be used for pupils to gather on arrival in the morning and again for departure when awaiting transport.

Music and drama

4.5 These are activities from which pupils with special needs can benefit greatly and wherever possible separate provision for music should be made, not only to allow the creation of one or more appropriate and dedicated spaces for those participating, but also to avoid distractions and disturbances to others. Drama activities involving the use of props, wardrobe, lighting and sound equipment can make a valuable contribution towards the development of pupils in special schools. Depending upon the number of pupils, their ages and the difficulties catered for, the provision could range from use of the school hall, where storage space will be necessary including perhaps storage for demountable stage units, to a separate facility also used for music or, in the largest secondary schools, a separate small hall.

Dining

4.6 Dining is a social and learning experience for many pupils with special needs. It is desirable for the complete school to eat together in an area which can be arranged in domestic-scale groupings. Isolated dining in class bases should be avoided wherever possible. Some pupils with profound and multiple learning difficulties may need individual attention and a great deal of time. Often various special diets are necessary and for this reason special schools usually have their own kitchens, even where different arrangements are the norm for ordinary schools in the area.

Sensory curriculum rooms, soft play rooms and pools

4.7 For many pupils with physical, learning and sensory difficulties there is a need for specialist facilities to help stimulate and develop responses. The three main types of provision are audio-visual rooms, soft play spaces and warm water pools, which can include splash, hydrotherapy and swimming pools. All of these facilities can have therapeutic effects and at the same time provide a learning environment.

Sensory curriculum rooms

4.8 These rooms can offer a range of experiences, including sight, sound, smell and touch, which are of value to pupils with severe and profound learning difficulties, sensory impairment and some physical disabilities. They will normally be used by a single pupil with a teacher, but sometimes by a small group of pupils with a teacher and, perhaps, an assistant.

4.9 In its simplest form the provision may be a small room from which daylight can be excluded, in which all surfaces are normally dark, and where the

Illustration 14
Music and Movement

tracking of moving lights can be undertaken. At the other of the scale are highly resourced rooms, often entirely white, although sometimes dark or multi-coloured, providing an environment of different sights, sounds and smells which can be activated individually or in concert by the teacher, the pupil, or both. Among the features which may be included are mirror balls, bubble tubes, wall mirrors, and fibre optics. Generally, although not necessarily, surfaces are soft, either carpet or foam, so that a pupil can lie and move about in comfort.

4.10   Allowance should be made for a considerable amount of electrical equipment, with extensive provision of socket outlets as well as efficient ventilation to deal with equipment heat emission. High-level shelving for some equipment, such as projectors, may be needed around the room. For the more advanced versions of this type of provision specialist advice should be sought.

Soft play rooms

4.11   In these rooms, which are invariably brightly multi-coloured, all the equipment and surfaces with which the

pupils may come into contact are soft and resilient, so that they can move about without inhibition or fear of injury. Lively and robust play is therefore encouraged which is particularly appropriate for younger pupils, especially those with severe and profound and multiple learning difficulties, but it can also be of benefit to pupils with sensory and certain physical difficulties.

4.12   A room of around 30m² is generally suitable, with all horizontal and vertical surfaces to a height of a metre or more covered with foam padding. The room may contain covered foam shapes such as cushions, wedges, steps and punchbags. Ball pools are sometimes provided. Natural light and ample natural ventilation are to be preferred. Window sills should be at least a metre above the foam floor surface and, unless the structural floor level is reduced to allow for the thickness of such covering, doors – which should also be padded – should open outwards. Foam can represent a particular fire hazard and the advice of the local fire authority should be sought. In an all-age school any soft play room should be located near class bases for the younger pupils, although it may also be used by some older pupils.

Illustration 15
Sensory stimulation room

fibre optics.

Regular cleaning of soft play equipment and ball pools will be necessary on hygiene grounds.

Warm water pools

4.13   Warm water pools are an effective medium for muscle relaxation, physical exercise, medical treatment and learning in an element where movement without great physical effort may be achieved, as well as offering a generally pleasurable and therapeutic experience. A pool is, however, an expensive facility and great care must be taken to ensure that its purpose is identified, and that an appropriate type of provision is specified in order that the facility will be fully used.

4.14   The splash pool has been a part of the provision of some special schools for a number of years*. Essentially it comprises a small, shallow pool appropriate for young pupils, the benefits of which are largely play and relaxation. It is likely to be of a size suitable for up to four pupils and the water depth is unlikely to be more than 300mm. Where water temperature and treatment are not controlled in conjunction with an adjacent larger pool, a splash pool may be filled and emptied like a bath, and water temperature maintained at an adequate level for the relatively short period of each session. When the pool is to be used by more than one pupil, water purification becomes important (see also para 4.18). A splash pool is of relatively limited benefit and does not present any opportunity for significant physical exercise or for medical treatment.

4.15   Hydrotherapy pools are increasingly being included in special schools, their use being principally for medical treatment and exercise. They are of benefit mainly for those with physical disabilities, and hydrotherapy may be specified on the statement for some pupils. Hydrotherapy pools are generally intended for up to three pupils at a time; the staff:pupil ratio is usually 1:1, the staff generally being in the pool with the pupils, although not always with older pupils who need less help. The water temperature needs to be 35°C, and air temperature 37°C. Many pools are custom-built to individual specifications, and are likely to be partially or wholly sunken. There are also proprietary types, usually prefabricated and installed to stand above floor level. Some may have glass sides to allow better observation.

4.16   Larger pools suitable for swimming are as useful for physical education in special schools as they are in ordinary schools, although additional features may be desirable for pupils

*See also *Design Note 10: Designing for the severely handicapped*[5].

Illustration 16
Soft play

with physical, learning and sensory difficulties. For example, underwater coloured lights which can be controlled by the teacher may be used to encourage responses not possible out of the water. The temperature should be 27–30°C with an air temperature 2°C higher.

4.17 It can be tempting with an expensive facility such as a pool to attempt to maximise its usefulness by providing for dual or multiple use, and this is particularly true in a special school where there is the need for both swimming and hydrotherapy. However, the two uses are virtually incompatible because of the difference in optimum water tempera-

ture. Temperatures appropriate for hydrotherapy are too high for swimming for more than a very limited distance or time, and to maintain such temperatures in the much greater volume of water in a swimming pool is unnecessarily expensive. Response times for water heating and cooling are too great for such pools to be really suitable for both activities. It is therefore essential that the purpose of any pool is clearly stated at briefing stage.

4.18 The planning and design of all pools should take account of the following considerations:

Figure 17
Hydrotherapy pool
A small pool suitable for up to three children in an area of 45m² plus store, toilet and changing area.

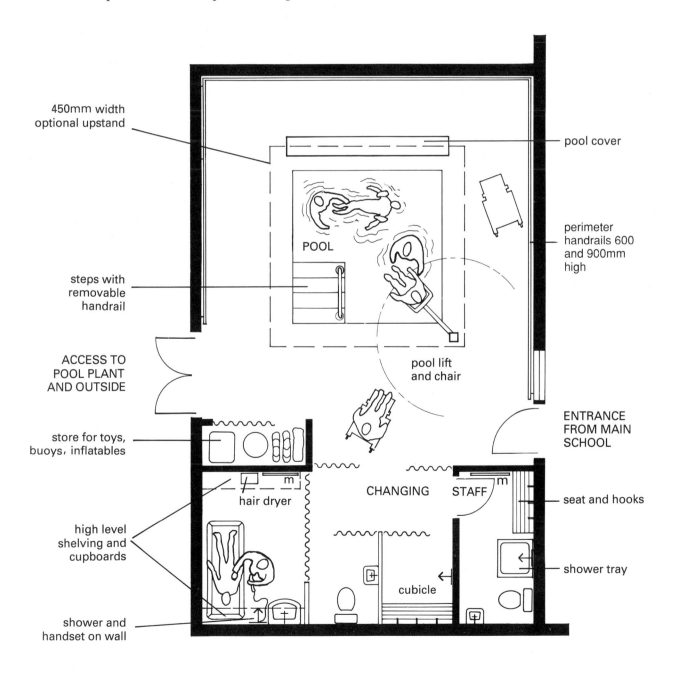

450mm width optional upstand

pool cover

POOL

perimeter handrails 600 and 900mm high

steps with removable handrail

ACCESS TO POOL PLANT AND OUTSIDE

pool lift and chair

ENTRANCE FROM MAIN SCHOOL

store for toys, buoys, inflatables

hair dryer

CHANGING   STAFF

seat and hooks

high level shelving and cupboards

cubicle

shower tray

shower and handset on wall

1   0   1   2   3   4m

• Whether the water level is to be at or below floor level or alternatively above, contained within a raised surround. In the latter case the surround can be broad enough to support a physically disabled pupil transferring or being transferred into the water by staff, whether from a wheelchair or not. In this way the pupil may be 'floated' into or out of the water without having to be lifted. Where the water surface is at or below floor level a ramped access may be provided. In both cases steps will also be needed.

• In schools for pupils with physical or profound and multiple learning difficulties, particularly those with secondary age pupils, hoists should be provided for lifting pupils into and out of the water. In view of the increasingly complex difficulties and disabilities of pupils in many schools such provision may be needed in all pools.

• The means of water purification needs particular consideration, not only because certain physical problems require that it be especially efficient, but also because some skin conditions may be aggravated by certain chemicals. Automatic rather than manual administration of the necessary chemicals is generally recommended, and the requirements of the local Environmental Health Officer will need to be met.

• The profile of the floor of the pool should allow for any change of water depth to be gradual. In small swimming pools this can be difficult to achieve.

• Lighting, both natural and artificial, should be carefully considered and located to avoid the problems which can be created by, for example, sunlight flickering across the water surface, which can be a problem for anyone subject to epilepsy. Vandalism is a factor to consider in deciding upon appropriate fenestration as broken glass in a pool involves considerable inconvenience and loss of the facility during the time taken to empty, clear and refill the pool.

• All pools need associated changing and toilet facilities which should include provision for the physically disabled, non-ambulant pupil.

• Specialist advice should be sought on the specification of finishes and the detailed design of the pool areas.

• The provision and siting of an alarm system should be considered so that staff can, if necessary, summon assistance if a pupil gets into difficulties in the pool.

4.19 The running costs of pools are substantial but may sometimes be par-

Illustration 17
Pool profiles

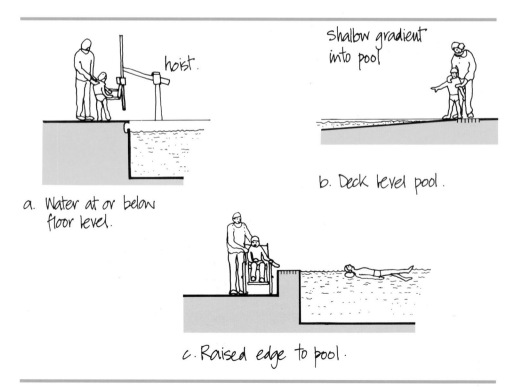

a. Water at or below floor level.

b. Deck level pool.

c. Raised edge to pool.

tially off-set by allowing use of the facilities by other schools and by community groups out of school hours. The provision should therefore be planned so that independent access is possible to the pool and associated areas.

Hygiene and toilet facilities

4.20   Careful briefing is needed to determine the extent and location of the provision required. The recommendations below are particularly appropriate to schools for pupils with profound and multiple learning difficulties and for those with physical difficulties, but some aspects will also apply to other special schools, especially as many are increasingly taking pupils with complex and multiple difficulties.

4.21   The acquisition of self-help and independence skills is a key area of the curriculum. Facilities must be large enough, with separate provision for different age groups and, for older pupils, different sexes. The balance between the sexes of pupils in individual special schools varies, and the design needs to take this into account. Teachers need to be able to create a suitable learning environment in areas which should be warm, bright and cheerful as well as hygienic and well-ventilated.

4.22   The maintenance of privacy and dignity for each pupil is very important. Many pupils in special schools will take time to achieve control of bowel and bladder functions, and facilities need to take account of this. Changing spaces are usually associated with other hygiene facilities, and consideration needs to be given to the privacy of each element within the unit. A number of dispersed areas close to teaching spaces will be needed, which can be reached easily and without having to cross major circulation routes or other rooms. This dispersal of facilities will inevitably tend to increase the extent of the provision required overall.

4.23   The location of hygiene and toilet facilities is crucial to the integration of pupils with profound and multiple or physical difficulties. A special care resource base with suitable and extensive provision may be needed. However, if pupils are to be able to join other groups and participate in all activities, provision elsewhere will also be necessary. When pupils with profound and multiple difficulties are to be fully integrated throughout a school where they comprise around a third or more of the total number, the hygiene facilities in each area will need to be more extensive.

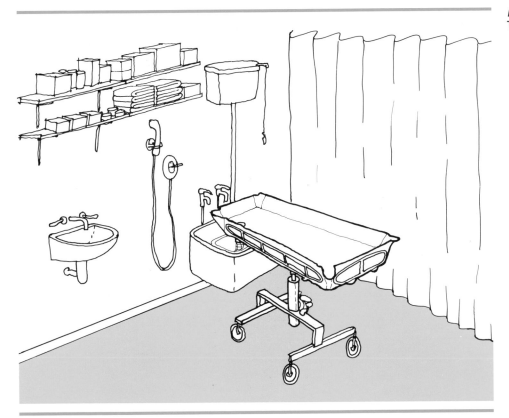

Illustration 18
Trolley for showering/changing

Figure 18
Hygiene and toilet areas
Provision which would be appropriate in schools for pupils with physical difficulties and for those with profound and multiple learning difficulties. Figures 18a and 18b are illustrated for secondary age pupils but similar provision would be needed for primary age pupils. In all hygiene areas there is storage shelving immediately to hand, and space for disposal bins is provided.

18a. An area opening off a secondary PMLD resource base which includes a laundry and is accessible from other parts of the building. Two WC compartments with alternative handing of the fittings are included, plus one with space at either side of the WC for use, for example, when two members of staff are assisting a pupil.

18b. Toilet and hygiene area in an SLD school where pupils with PMLD are integrated with other pupils. It assumes a PMLD resource base plus hygiene area elsewhere in the school and provides a single hygiene/ changing space. This includes a WC and washhand basin handed differently from those in the adjacent wheelchair-accessible compartments. The WC/ hygiene room would be for use by only one pupil at a time.

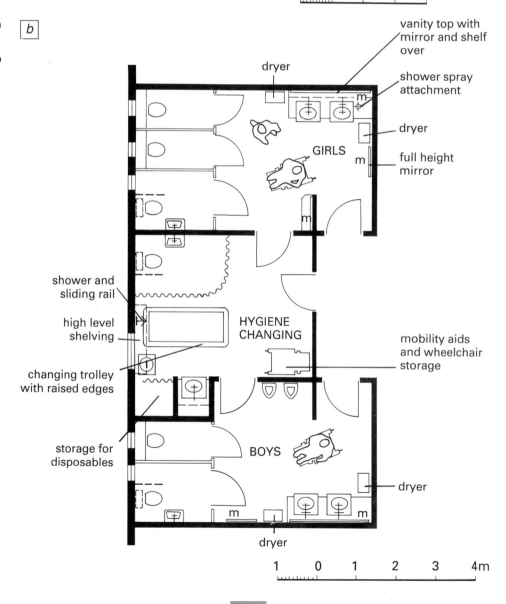

a

ACCESS FROM PMLD BASE
mobility aid
ST
high level windows
m
changing trolley with raised edges over sluice
storage shelf at high level
rooflight
hoist over bath
personal items in individual compartments
WM
D LAUNDRY
ST
ST
ACCESS FROM OTHER AREAS

1 0 1 2 3 m

b

dryer
vanity top with mirror and shelf over
shower spray attachment
dryer
GIRLS
m
full height mirror
m
shower and sliding rail
high level shelving
HYGIENE CHANGING
mobility aids and wheelchair storage
changing trolley with raised edges
storage for disposables
BOYS
dryer
m
dryer
m

1 0 1 2 3 4m

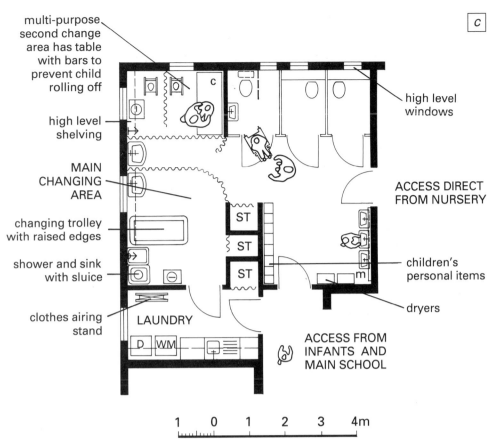

multi-purpose second change area has table with bars to prevent child rolling off

high level shelving

MAIN CHANGING AREA

changing trolley with raised edges

shower and sink with sluice

clothes airing stand

LAUNDRY

high level windows

ACCESS DIRECT FROM NURSERY

children's personal items

dryers

ACCESS FROM INFANTS AND MAIN SCHOOL

C

18c. Toilet and hygiene area, with laundry, opening off a nursery and with access also from infants' class bases. Besides the main hygiene/changing space there is a second area which could be divided by means of curtains to provide cubicle-size areas for training chairs for those pupils not yet using WCs. All WC cubicles are large enough for staff assistance.

1   0   1   2   3   4m

WC fittings and compartments

4.24   Like all new schools, special schools should provide for the physically disabled. Appropriate wheelchair-accessible compartments should be available for pupils and, separately, for staff and other adults. When planning new accommodation an integrated range of cubicles for both ambulant and wheelchair users should be considered. When adapting existing buildings separate wheelchair-accessible provision may have to be made.

4.25   Some pupils, including both ambulant and wheelchair users, and especially the under-sevens, may need staff assistance for which sufficient space must be allowed. Other pupils, including those using wheelchairs, may be independent and for them the type of compartment with support rails and adjacent washhand basin generally to be found in public buildings would be suitable. Support rails which fold up against the wall when not needed can be useful. For some pupils with physical difficulties the direction of approach to the fitting may be important. Thus, wherever possible, alternatives should be

offered. In some cases space for access and assistance from both sides may be necessary and a compartment large enough to allow for the presence of two adults with a large pupil and a wheelchair may be necessary. In some cases mechanical assistance with lifting will be needed and may involve the use of mobile hoists. Where possible pipework, cisterns, mixer valves, etc should be boxed-in to render them tamper-proof and to provide easily cleaned surfaces. However, where side transfer from a wheelchair is involved there needs to be space between the back of the WC pan and the wall behind, and this space should not be enclosed. Depending upon the age range of the school, and especially when there is a nursery, some difference in WC heights may be desirable. Efficient ventilation of all such areas is essential.

4.26   Some pupils may not have acquired head and trunk control and may need support in order to use conventional toilet facilities. There are a number of commercially produced fittings which can be attached to WCs to provide support for the trunk, neck and feet. Where pupils need still greater support, chair commodes may be suitable. Commodes should be located adjacent to changing and disposal facilities and placed so as to ensure privacy for the user. Space for storing such aids and fittings when not in use will be required.

Washhand basins and personal care

4.27   Facilities for washing hands and face and for brushing teeth should be available in close proximity to WCs. The heights of washhand basins should be suitable for those standing and for those in wheelchairs, and again some age differentiation may be desirable. Mirrors and shelves should be related to the basin height. Vanity units and facilities for washing hair may be appropriate where this is not provided elsewhere, for example in a life skills area. Wall-mounted hair dryers may be included. Choice of taps will depend on whether the priority is to suit a particular type of disability or to provide practice in using those most likely to be encountered elsewhere. All taps and showers to which pupils have access should deliver water at a temperature between 38°C and 42°C. The storage of all personal items such as towels and toothbrushes must prevent any chance of cross-contamination.

Showering, bathing and changing

4.28   Access to a shower or bath for washing pupils and a sluice for the

disposal of soil is often necessary, together with hygienic arrangements for the storage and disposal of soiled dressings and clothing. Mobile, height-adjustable trolleys suitable for both showering and changing can be safer for both pupils and staff than a fixed-height changing table and can discharge directly over a sluice. Positioning should allow for assistance from at least two sides. At times there may be more than one adult assisting so that the pupil can be changed quickly and safely. For the health and safety of both pupils and staff, mechanical assistance with lifting may be needed where there are large and heavy pupils. Shelving for storing toiletries, clean dressings and clothing should be provided within arm's reach of the changing table or trolley, and hand washing facilities for staff should be immediately available. Storage for day-to-day supplies of disposable items will be required, although bulk storage may be provided elsewhere in the building. Space is also needed for temporarily unused wheelchairs and other aids, and perhaps for disposal bins.

4.29   In some schools there may be a need for simple showering and changing provision adjacent to teaching areas. Here it may be sufficient to include a shower, perhaps in an enlarged WC compartment, including a washhand basin, but not necessarily space for a changing trolley or table. Provision of this type may be suitable in some

Illustration 19
Bathroom with hoist

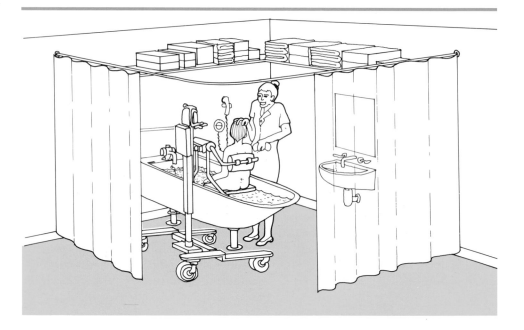

schools for pupils with moderate learning difficulties or emotional and behavioural difficulties.

Stoma care

4.30   There may be pupils who require access to a facility for changing appliances. This may be provided as part of the medical treatment area where adequate privacy and hygiene can be provided, together with assistance and training. For pupils able to care for themselves facilities can conveniently be provided in larger wheelchair-accessible WC compartments, or as part of the changing area. The essential requirement is for drainage, sterilisation and storage of tubes and bags, and the storage of dressings and toiletries.

Laundry

4.31   In schools where incontinence may be a problem a laundry for the washing and drying of clothes will also be needed. This will usually be located off the nursery or special care resource area but should also be accessible from other areas of the building. Machines may be commercial or domestic depending on the amount of use, but should not be located in a home economics area or combined with any kitchen use.

Bases for therapists and other visiting specialists

4.32   Pupils and teaching staff are supported by specialists such as physiotherapists, speech and language therapists, occupational therapists and psychologists, who may be full-time or may visit a number of schools. The extent of their accommodation varies according to the pupils' needs. Therapy now tends to be delivered in the teaching situation, with teacher and therapist working together. This has the advantage that the teacher or special support assistant can continue the therapy while the therapist is elsewhere. However, some therapy still needs to be carried out away from the class group. Provision for this will range from an office shared by different specialists, where equipment can be kept and administrative work done, to special separate rooms suitably equipped and resourced for work with pupils, either individually or in small groups.

Physiotherapy

4.33   In many schools the provision of adequate floor space in the classroom, and simple equipment, such as full body mirrors, enable a physiotherapist to work in the classroom with the teacher.

Illustration 20
Physiotherapy session in class

However, any rooms provided specifically for physiotherapy will need to be sufficiently large to provide for the specialised equipment in use, generally by one therapist, although there may be two working from time to time in larger schools for pupils with physical difficulties. Space will be needed for working with floor mats, large inflatables, parallel bars, and other large items, with adequate space around them. A working area of at least 15m², unencumbered by storage, is needed for one physiotherapist. Wall space is necessary for fixed equipment such as mirrors and wall bars, and for display. Much of the equipment will need to be moved out from storage areas, and therefore sufficient accessible storage is needed in addition to the usable room area (about one-third of its area). The room should have natural light and a pleasant aspect. It should be located close to the teaching areas of the school to reduce any withdrawal time to a minimum and to facilitate the physiotherapist and teacher working together. There should be easy access to the toilet and hygiene facilities. To allow for larger-scale physical activity easy access is also desirable to a large space such as a hall or gymnasium.

Occupational therapy

4.34   In many special schools support is available from occupational therapists to help pupils overcome physical difficul-

ties. This work is usually best carried out in the classroom in conjunction with the teacher or other responsible adult. The space required to accommodate activity and equipment for the development of independent living skills, in addition to that for use by all staff, may need to be expanded in those schools catering for older pupils. Some administrative work will be necessary, and can be adequately provided for by the shared use of office space.

Speech and language therapy

4.35   Many special schools are at present provided by the health authority with support by speech and language therapists, either full-time or part-time. Much of the work is in the classroom. Where withdrawal from the class is necessary, accommodation can often be found in small group rooms or quiet rooms, provided good acoustic separation is possible. Such withdrawal work normally requires no specialist facilities. In some special schools speech and language therapy is a very significant part of the curriculum, for example schools for the hearing impaired, or for pupils with speech and language problems. The speech and language therapist needs a base in which to store equipment and records, plan and prepare programmes and in which pupils can be assessed or taught, if necessary. The base should have a high degree of sound

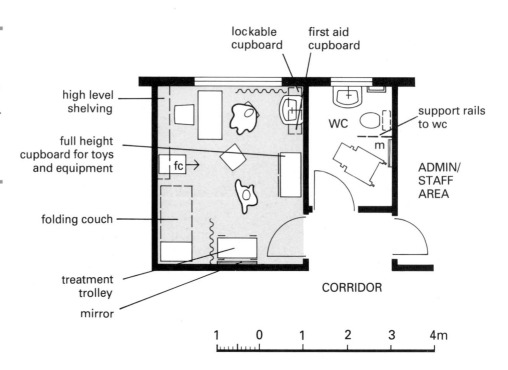

Figure 19
Medical room
The provision shown would be suitable for a small school for pupils without significant physical difficulties and might be used also by visiting specialists. If used as a rest room or for a sick pupil with no medical staff present it could be supervised from an adjacent permanently staffed area.

lockable cupboard

first aid cupboard

high level shelving

full height cupboard for toys and equipment

fc

folding couch

treatment trolley

mirror

WC

support rails to wc

m

ADMIN/ STAFF AREA

CORRIDOR

1   0   1   2   3   4m

insulation from adjacent spaces because high noise levels are likely. The criteria for reverberation time and sound absorption depend upon the equipment used, being most stringent for audiology.

Educational psychology

4.36   Most special schools are supported by a visiting psychologist and much of the work is in the classroom. Access may be required to suitable interview space for a family group, but for most schools this could be a shared space. Provision for administration is necessary, and can be adequately provided for by shared use of an office.

Medical facilities

4.37   All schools require a medical room for the treatment and care of pupils and for visiting medical staff. This room should be sited to allow for close supervision of a sick pupil by a member of staff and it is therefore usually located next to the administrative accommodation. It should have a washbasin and be near a lavatory. Some special schools will, however, need more extensive provision, normally one or more special rooms suitably furnished and equipped, for use by clinical and nursing staff. Sometimes – for example

at schools for pupils with emotional and behavioural difficulties or moderate learning difficulties – this facility can be shared with other specialists such as speech and language therapists. Special requirements may arise from the nature of the pupils for whom the school caters, for example visually impaired pupils, where there will be a visiting ophthalmologist and control of natural and artificial light may be necessary. The design and specification of the structure and of doors and windows should provide good soundproofing as, in most schools, hearing tests will be conducted in the medical room.

4.38   In a school for pupils with physical difficulties, or for one including a number of pupils with profound and multiple difficulties, there may be full-time nursing staff, and early consultations with the health authority are essential when formulating the brief.

4.39   In even the simplest medical room provision must be made for vision testing, examination, the safe disposal of contaminated waste and washing. Lockable storage should be provided for drugs, within which there should be separate lockable storage for dangerous drugs. Rooms in which drugs are kept should not normally be accessible to pupils. There should be natural light and ventilation.

Illustration 21
Resource/preparation area for staff

Technicians' rooms

4.40 Some schools for pupils in which technical aids are intensively used, such as those for pupils with sensory difficulties, have technicians responsible for the maintenance and repair of visual and auditory aids carried out in the school. Where such a service is provided there is a need for a room with natural light and ventilation, fitted with practical benching, secure storage and open shelving, and adequate electrical services. Water and gas services will not normally be required for work on electrical or electronic equipment, but may be necessary in schools where other equipment is to be repaired and maintained.

Staff accommodation

4.41 Staff need adequate space both for work preparation and meetings and for social purposes at breaks and lunchtime. A staff room should be provided which has sufficient space and furniture for each adult who works regularly in the school to plan lessons and produce learning resources, to relax comfortably and to keep personal effects secure. The staff room may also be used regularly for whole staff meetings. There should be notice boards and storage of publica-

tions staff may wish to read. There should be facilities for making refreshments, either within the staff room or immediately adjacent to it. Space is also required to enable small groups of staff to meet to plan the curriculum, for internal case conferences, or for review meetings.

4.42 Where the special school is a centre for the support of special educational needs in surrounding schools additional accommodation will be needed, for example an office with facilities for the storage of records and teaching materials and equipment. A large meeting/ working room may be required when there are peripatetic teachers based at the school. Photocopying facilities are needed and audio and video materials will often have to be collated and stored. For pupils with visual impairment technical equipment for producing braille or tactile materials and enlarging print is required. Frequently a special support assistant or technician may work full-time in these areas producing learning materials both for the special school and for pupils in local ordinary schools.

4.43 A room is required for the head teacher. It should be sufficiently large to

Figure 20
Staff accommodation: diagrammatic location plan
The staff room is located centrally, with easy access to teaching areas and pool, so that rapid assistance may be summoned if staff and/or pupils are in difficulty. Physiotherapy is located with easy access to the hall, pool and class bases. Visiting specialists' rooms may also be used for case conferences and other discussions. The head's room and administration area are located close to the entrance and adjacent to the medical/rest room.

KEY

A Staff room:
   relaxation and meetings

B Staff room:
   work and resources

C Administration:
   Head and secretary

D Visiting specialists

E Physiotherapy

F Staff toilets

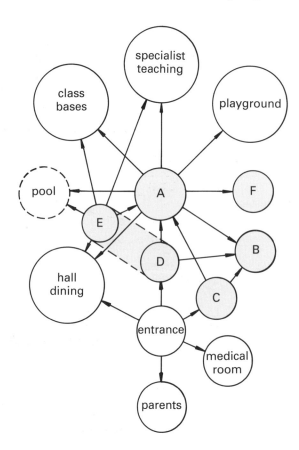

permit interviews with a small group, for example a teacher and a pupil with parents, in secure acoustic conditions. It should be located with easy access to the school's administrative accommodation, and close to the principal entrance. A room for the deputy head is also required.

4.44   The small size of many special schools means that full-time secretarial support may not be available. Provision may need to range from accommodating one or two part-time staff, to two or three full-time. It will always be helpful if the location of the school office is close to the main entrance and its reception function is recognised.

Parents' facilities

4.45   Most special schools benefit from space set aside for parents to meet informally and socially. There should be comfortable seating and provision for the making of refreshments.

4.46   It is helpful if direct access off a circulation space is possible. Parents may assist in the school from time to time and may also visit the school to work with the staff on their child's particular difficulty. The growth of these mutually beneficial relationships between school and parents can be encouraged if space is provided for social purposes, for small meetings and for occasional work with pupil, parent and teacher or therapist.

Storage

4.47   Teaching storage may range from storage furniture within the classroom to separate walk-in stores. The choice will depend upon the age of the pupils, the nature of the learning difficulty, and the appropriate teaching method. Some schools for secondary pupils with emotional and behavioural difficulties may wish to control pupils' access to learning material and lockable walk-in storage will be the more appropriate. Other

Figure 21
Parents' room
The room shown would be suitable for a small school. It is located off the entrance and provides an informal space for discussion and relaxation, with facilities for making hot drinks. It also includes space for storing and displaying information and for some desk work.

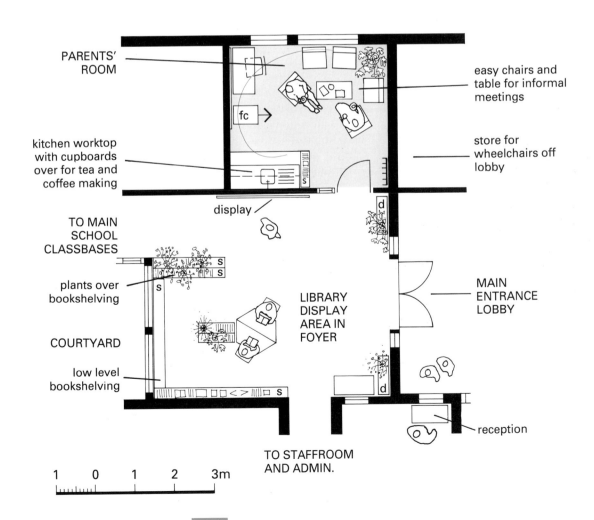

PARENTS' ROOM

kitchen worktop with cupboards over for tea and coffee making

fc →

s

easy chairs and table for informal meetings

store for wheelchairs off lobby

display

d

TO MAIN SCHOOL CLASSBASES

plants over bookshelving

s
s
s

COURTYARD

low level bookshelving

s

LIBRARY DISPLAY AREA IN FOYER

MAIN ENTRANCE LOBBY

d

reception

TO STAFFROOM AND ADMIN.

1   0   1   2   3m

schools will wish to allow pupils immediate access to a wide range of learning material, and the provision of open access shelving within the classroom will be beneficial. Schools for pupils with severe learning difficulties usually require open access storage complemented by walk-in storage for a range of bulky items that are used only occasionally.

4.48 In addition to conventional learning materials, many special schools will need to provide storage for learning aids in use by the pupils, for example braille machines, or special keyboards. Schools for the visually impaired that are using braille have particular requirements for the bulk storage of braille documents.

4.49 Teaching storage will also be needed for specialist teaching areas such as science, design technology, art and physical education. This will normally be provided as in ordinary schools, except that because the full range of subject teaching materials will be provided for only one or two teaching spaces the proportionate area of storage may be greater. Where multi-use spaces are required each function should be supported by separate storage.

4.50 Adequate central bulk storage should be provided of a size related to delivery periods for teaching materials.

4.51 Storage will also be needed for non-teaching materials: the central storage of bulk caretaker's supplies, the local storage of cleaning materials, and the storage of materials related to the administrative accommodation. Since much of these materials is hazardous, particular care is needed in the provision of safe storage.

4.52 Schools for pupils with physical difficulties and profound and multiple difficulties will also need space for the bulk storage of napkins and sanitary towels, as well as for the local storage of small quantities of these items within the sanitary facilities. The bulk storage requirement will be related to supply periods. Such schools are also likely to need clothes storage in or near a laundry.

4.53 There is a major storage requirement for wheelchairs, walking frames, callipers, and other mobility aids. These aids are in use from time to time and from place to place in the school, and pupils may well use two or three such

Illustration 22
Parents' room

aids during the course of the day. Sufficient local storage space should therefore be available in and adjacent to teaching areas. In addition storage space is needed adjacent to where pupils enter the school because the mobility aid used for getting to school is often not used during the course of the day. Any overnight wheelchair storage should make provision for battery charging, with appropriate arrangements for ventilation.

4.54 Many special schools are equipped with a considerable quantity of valuable items such as computers, television sets, tape recorders, etc. Because of the quantities involved, and their wide distribution about the school, collection into a single high-security store at the end of the day becomes difficult. Local storage provided as part of teaching storage can be effectively

used. It should be lockable with good quality ironmongery and substantial joinery. However, protection will be mainly by virtue of the school's security system. A safe should be provided within the administrative accommodation.

4.55 A range of storage needs arises from activities outside the building. Schools with young pupils, or older pupils with severe, including profound and multiple, learning difficulties, will use play equipment in the areas immediately outside their class bases. Therefore stores for bulky items, such as sand and water tables, tricycles and portable slides, are desirable, with access from both inside and outdoors. Similar considerations apply to the storage of equipment for physical education, some of which will be used both inside and outdoors.

Illustration 23
Wheelchair store

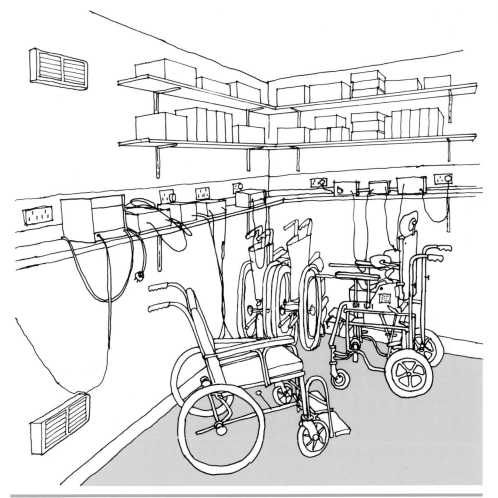

Location

5.1   This is generally determined by the special needs of the pupils for whom the school is to provide, the catchment area and the proposed extent of links with the surrounding community. In deciding upon a suitable location for a new school the following factors should be taken into consideration.

Catchment area

5.2   This is often much greater than for an ordinary school. Schools for pupils with learning difficulties usually serve a fairly local population with the pupils living within daily travelling distance, but the much smaller number of schools for pupils with sensory impairment are beyond the daily reach of many pupils

Figure 22
Diagrammatic location plan
This indicates a location close to an ordinary school which caters for a similar age range and within an area suitable for the development of community links.

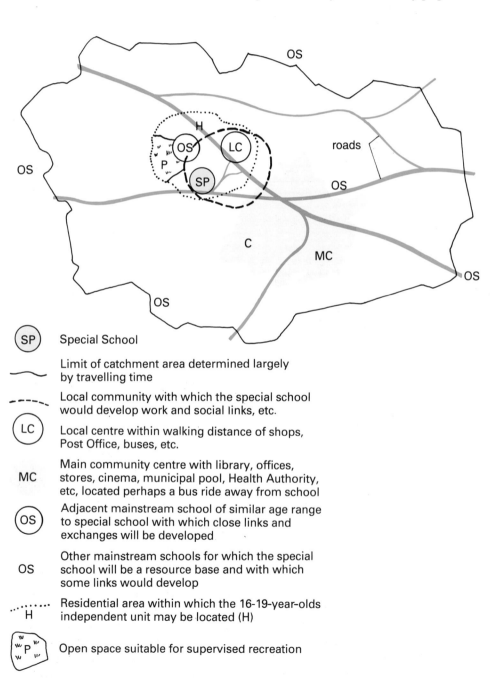

(SP)	Special School
⌇	Limit of catchment area determined largely by travelling time
- - - - -	Local community with which the special school would develop work and social links, etc.
(LC)	Local centre within walking distance of shops, Post Office, buses, etc.
MC	Main community centre with library, offices, stores, cinema, municipal pool, Health Authority, etc, located perhaps a bus ride away from school
(OS)	Adjacent mainstream school of similar age range to special school with which close links and exchanges will be developed
OS	Other mainstream schools for which the special school will be a resource base and with which some links would develop
······· H	Residential area within which the 16-19-year-olds independent unit may be located (H)
P	Open space suitable for supervised recreation
C	College

and are therefore often residential. In the case of day schools, the amount of travelling time has to be borne in mind, together with easy access by public transport. Considerable parental involvement in the life of a special school is likely to be encouraged, but sometimes will be possible only if the site is easily accessible by public transport. Residential special schools may provide weekly boarding, in which case the travelling time at weekends is again a significant factor. For those offering termly or 52-week boarding, travelling times are less important, but parents still need to visit, and not all own cars.

Traffic considerations

5.3   Most pupils are brought to school either by bus, ambulance, taxi or car and this generates a significant volume of traffic at certain times of the day. The choice of location and the planning of the site should take account of the impact this may have on the immediate neighbourhood. For safety reasons vehicles should not need to be reversed in the vicinity of the site.

Social, educational and employment links

5.4   For many pupils the curriculum is likely to include everyday occupations such as shopping and using public transport. Thus a location close to community activities is an advantage. Contacts with local residents, organisations and businesses can lead to them taking an active interest in the school. Involvement may extend to the pupils' welfare, to shared social activities and use of facilities, to job and training opportunities and to service in the community. The school may wish to develop off-site accommodation so that older pupils can practise independence. This might be a house or flat in the local community.

5.5   For many pupils attending a special school the aim will be to enter, or return to, mainstream education, on a full- or part-time basis. This will be facilitated if the special school is sited near to ordinary schools with which educational and social links can be developed. For many older pupils in special schools, college links and an increasing time away from the school will be normal.

The special school as a resource centre

5.6   With the increasing integration of pupils with special needs in ordinary schools, the special school may provide a base of staff expertise and material resources which would not otherwise be available to the individual pupil in an ordinary school. A supply of equipment, aids and technical support is often built up and available on loan, particularly in the case of schools for pupils with visual and hearing impairment. It is therefore an advantage for a special school to be located where it can conveniently support pupils in a number of ordinary schools in the area.

The site

5.7   School grounds can be an immensely valuable resource for extending learning as well as for recreation. External works often receive a low priority at the briefing stage and may be the first area to suffer when savings are sought. This can result in under-used and utilitarian outside areas. Yet the imaginative planning and design of hard and soft landscaping can greatly enhance the potential for rich and varied educational opportunities as well as improving the appearance of the school and the way in which it is perceived by users, visitors and the neighbouring community. In this context reference should also be made to DES *Building Bulletin 71: The Outdoor Classroom*[6].

5.8   Accessibility is a major consideration which should apply to the choice of site and the design of external areas for most special schools. For pupils with physical difficulties a steeply sloping site would clearly be inappropriate, but this does not mean that all changes of level should be avoided. Exploitation of variations in level where these already exist, and earth modelling where they do not, can contribute to the creation of an interesting and useful variety of spaces. In many schools land which might otherwise be bleak and under-used can be greatly improved by the imaginative use of levels and planting. This can help to create sheltered and welcoming spaces, ideal for learning and play. Pupils with physical and sensory difficulties can benefit from an element of challenge which helps to develop independence and self-confidence. Planting and changes of level can also serve to reduce the impact of utilitarian areas such as those for car parking.

5.9 The safety of the pupils is crucial and, as with ordinary schools and particularly those for younger pupils, a degree of containment is likely to be desirable, both to prevent the pupils from straying and to avoid unauthorised access. The layout should segregate vehicle access, including service access, from the outdoor areas used by pupils during the day. For some pupils, such as those with behavioural difficulties, running away can be a problem. Nevertheless, the nature of a site enclosure should not be oppressive.

5.10 Design and planning should take account of the possibility of vandalism out of school hours. In considering the benefits of creating sheltered spaces around the building perimeter, the opportunities which such areas offer to intruders must also be recognised. Reference should be made to DES *Building Bulletin 67: Crime prevention in schools: practical guidance*[7].

Access

5.11 Direct access to the building is generally necessary for vehicles such as minibuses as well as for private cars and taxis, and this means adequate provision must be made for turning, waiting and passing. There should be a one-way flow which avoids any need for reversing. A layout suitable for vehicles up to about 8m in length is usually sufficient, although requirements need to be established from the outset, as sometimes access for full-size coaches may be needed. Pupils with mobility and other difficulties may need considerable time for getting into and out of vehicles and this should, if possible, take place under cover. A canopy under which vehicles can stand and which then leads directly into the building is therefore recom-

Figure 23
Site plan
The layout shown separates vehicle areas from those which can be accessed by the pupils from within the building. It assumes a small all-age school (pupils up to the age of 16) with a nursery which links with the main school but might also have its own independent access. The extent of the outdoor provision would be appropriate for an SLD or PD school.

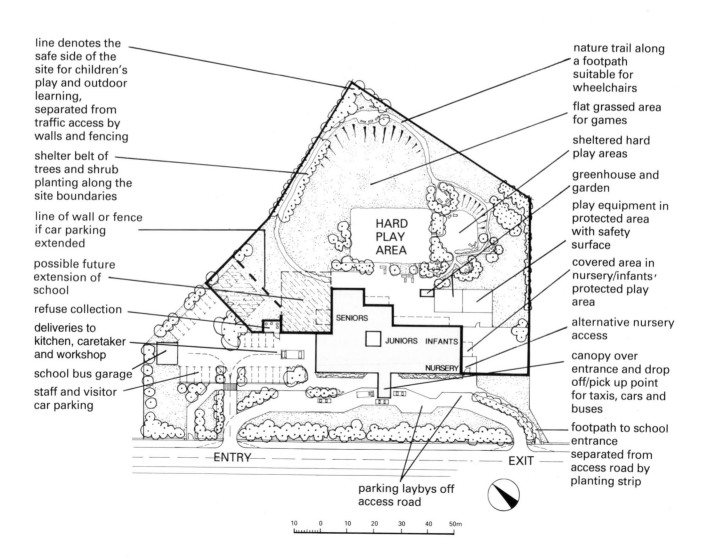

mended. As in all schools, disability and dependence on vehicle access should not necessitate the use of an entrance different from that used by others. Such access should therefore be to the main entrance, not to some side or service entrance.

5.12 Although most, and often all, pupils will use vehicles, care must be taken to provide a safe pedestrian route to the entrance which does not involve crossing setting-down areas. Footpaths suitable to the needs of the pupils are required around the site to link and give access to all facilities provided for them.

5.13 Parking areas, while clearly belonging to the approach side of the site, should whenever possible be located away from the setting-down area, and should not encroach on hard play areas. Since it will usually be necessary to provide one car parking space for each full-time member of staff, plus provision for the many visiting specialists and others, car parking areas are likely to be large. Ingenuity in planning and design will be needed to reduce their visual impact, by means of screening, levels and planting. A school may have its own minibus or buses for which a garage will be needed, again preferably away from the setting-down area.

5.14 Any vehicle access to extend around the building should be for emergency use only. Service access for delivery vehicles to the kitchen, for the caretaker's supplies and to boiler and plant rooms should where possible be kept separate from the main setting-down area and must not extend into areas used by pupils. Access for refuse vehicles should be confined to service areas, but may not be needed within the site perimeter at all if bin stores can be suitably located. These should be convenient for, but not necessarily adjacent to, the kitchen. In many special schools there may also be contaminated and medical waste, and this will need safe storage and special disposal arrangements.

Outdoor teaching

5.15 External spaces can provide opportunities for observation, investigation and problem-solving and form a flexible facility often more readily adaptable to changes in user requirements than the building itself. They can offer a stimulating environment suited to practical activities from which many pupils with special needs can benefit.

5.16 Class bases for younger pupils in particular should open directly out onto a space which can be used as an easily supervised extension of the classroom. It should be possible to move equipment and resources readily between the two and there should be access to bulk storage space. The provision of covered space giving protection from inclement weather considerably extends the length of time such areas may be used, particularly for younger pupils and those who

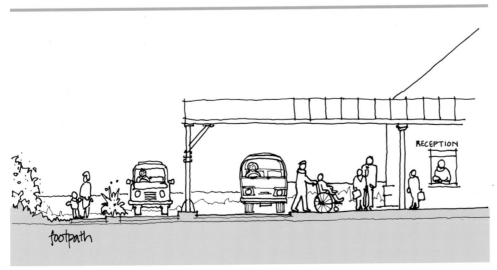

Illustration 24
Setting down under cover

may be physically vulnerable. Verandahs, where they can be deep enough without significantly reducing daylight levels in the classroom, can be useful. Alternatively, projecting open-sided canopies can provide more extensive areas without running the length of the window wall.

5.17   Nursery outdoor areas usually have a perimeter enclosure to provide protection, and this should also allow views out. Within this space there should be both hard and soft surfaces, with sufficient space for bulky play equipment, both fixed and mobile. Sand and water play are likely to be included, and where these are permanent features attention must be paid to safety and hygiene. Sand pits should be covered when not in use and any pool perimeter must be designed, so far as is possible, to prevent accidents. Safety surfaces are necessary under equipment such as

climbing frames, both in the nursery area and elsewhere. Reference should also be made to *Playground Safety Guidelines*[8].

5.18   Courtyards can be especially useful for outdoor teaching if they are large enough and suitably orientated. Increasingly, covered courtyards are being included in special school designs. These are generally unheated spaces providing protection from the weather and are used for either teaching or recreation. Again, orientation and detailed design are important to ensure they receive adequate daylight and some sunshine, but without excessive solar gain in summer.

5.19   Outdoor spaces both adjacent to the building and at a distance from it can be suitable for work in a wide variety of subjects. Among the most obvious is horticulture, and a garden area, includ-

Figure 24
Protected nursery play area
An enclosed space into which the nursery opens and to which infant classes might also have access. Area adjacent to the base covered.

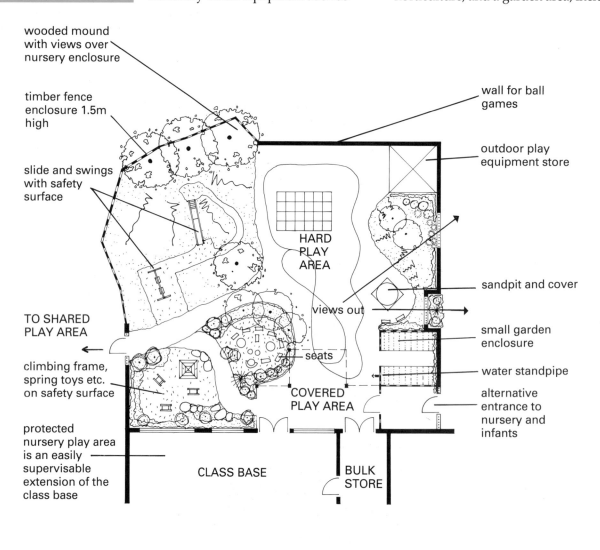

wooded mound with views over nursery enclosure

timber fence enclosure 1.5m high

slide and swings with safety surface

TO SHARED PLAY AREA

climbing frame, spring toys etc. on safety surface

protected nursery play area is an easily supervisable extension of the class base

wall for ball games

outdoor play equipment store

HARD PLAY AREA

views out

sandpit and cover

small garden enclosure

water standpipe

alternative entrance to nursery and infants

seats

COVERED PLAY AREA

CLASS BASE

BULK STORE

N

1 0 1 2 3 4 5 6 7m

ing raised beds suitable for pupils in wheelchairs, and possibly a greenhouse, will often be associated with the specialist practical teaching areas of the school. For pupils with various difficulties, and especially visual impairment, a small herb garden or fragrant shrubs and flowers may be appreciated. Where space allows, the creation of a wildlife garden and/or a 'nature trail' may be possible. For primary age pupils outdoor spaces, including courtyards, may provide an opportunity for looking after and observing animals. However, the site can also offer opportunities to pursue studies, in class groups and more independently, related to almost all curriculum subjects, from art and design technology through science to mathematics and English, as outlined in *Building Bulletin 71*[6].

5.20 School sites for pupils with physical and sensory difficulties should make provision for mobility and independence training. For visually impaired pupils a variety of surfaces and com-

monplace features may be included. Horizontal and vertical surfaces may be treated to help identify location using texture, acoustic quality, air pressure changes and other sensory stimuli. Pupils with physical difficulties can benefit if part of the site is designed to familiarise them with safety precautions and overcoming obstacles likely to be encountered in the outside world.

5.21 Sport and physical education are an essential part of the curriculum, and the land requirements may affect the assessment of the suitability of a potential special school site. Schools for pupils with moderate learning difficulties need facilities similar to those of an ordinary school, including playing fields for team games. Provided the pupils attending the special school receive a fair share of allocated time, it may be possible for such provision to be shared with another, often mainstream, school. This can be a good thing in itself, and particularly helpful in the case of a small school, such as one for pupils with

Figure 25
Courtyard
A small outdoor space for relaxation or group teaching. Section through raised pond with safety rail shows change of ground surface texture which would alert pupils with visual impairment to the location.

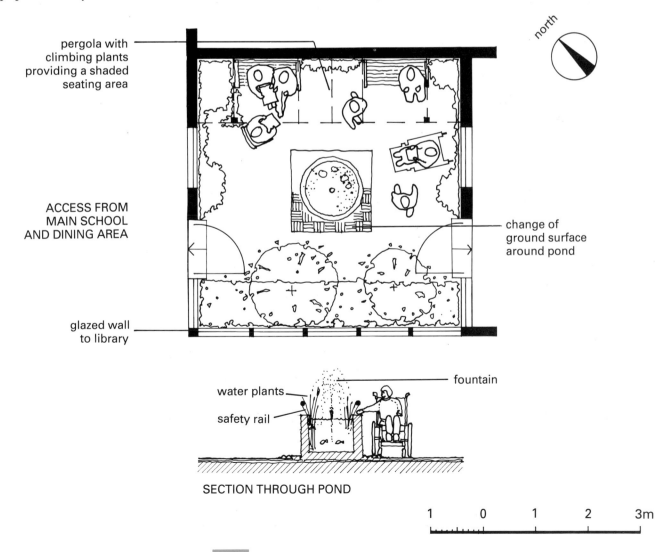

pergola with climbing plants providing a shaded seating area

ACCESS FROM MAIN SCHOOL AND DINING AREA

glazed wall to library

change of ground surface around pond

north

fountain

water plants

safety rail

SECTION THROUGH POND

1 0 1 2 3m

emotional and behavioural difficulties, where the numbers may be insufficient to fully use the playing field. Schools for pupils with physical or severe and profound learning difficulties will need some hard- and soft-surfaced playing areas, but large-scale team games are less likely to be played. Areas for perhaps five-a-side games, which can also be marked out for bicycle routes and agility games such as hopscotch etc, are likely to be suitable. There should still be sufficient area for pupils to enjoy races and boisterous games, whether on foot or in wheelchairs, and so a level area will be needed. Activities appropriate to the particular difficulties should be allowed for, such as archery for some pupils who may be wheelchair bound.

Recreation

5.22   Recreation spaces are essential. Most play will take place on the open areas provided for games, but where there are pupils who may be physically vulnerable there is a need for some smaller, more sheltered spaces. Ideally such more protected spaces will link with the main playground and open onto it. Shelter may be provided by

means of planting as well as by low walls and banks. Seating will usually be included. Planning and specification need to take into account the fact that today many pupils operate electric chairs and buggies at speeds of 5 mph and more. Areas to which pupils may have independent access should generally be capable of being easily supervised by staff. For some pupils access to other areas may need to be controlled, and this would apply particularly where there is a potential danger, such as a pond.

5.23   Playbarns of simple and relatively low-cost construction can sometimes compensate for limited sports facilities within a small school and can also provide recreation space which can be used in all weathers.

Future development

5.24   Changing expectations and requirements make it almost inevitable that over the years some extension of the building will become necessary. The size of the site and the layout of the building and other provision should make some allowance for this.

Illustration 25
Raised garden beds for wheelchair access

Environmental services

5.25   The guidance given in *Design Note 17: Guidelines for environmental design and fuel conservation in educational buildings*[9] includes many of the requirements relevant to special schools, in particular those relating to heating, lighting, ventilation and energy consumption. Other factors that need consideration are discussed in *Design Note 25*[4]. The following notes are pointers to the factors that will need to be considered in any special school.

Heating

5.26   Room design temperatures need to take into account the needs of the pupils. For those schools in which the activity rate of pupils is not affected by their difficulty, for example schools for pupils with moderate learning difficulty, emotional and behavioural difficulty or visual or hearing impairment, teaching room temperatures can be as for ordinary schools, that is 18°C. In schools where some pupils may have very low activity rates and some may be non-ambulant, special consideration is necessary and the temperature of teaching spaces should be 21°C. This would apply to schools for pupils with physical difficulties and those with profound and multiple learning difficulties. However, as pupils in special schools tend to have more complex needs, special schools generally should be designed so that the necessary higher temperatures can be achieved if required.

5.27   A consequence of the increasing level of difficulty of the pupils in special schools is that nearly all have rooms in which pupils are likely to be unclothed, or partially clothed and perhaps wet, for significant periods of time, for example for medical inspection, changing, bathing, etc. Comfortable conditions in such circumstances depend on both temperature and air speed (see *CIBSE Guide*, Section A1, Environmental criteria for design[10]), and design temperatures are likely to range between 25°C and 30°C. Rapid air movement leads to chilling by evaporation, therefore air speed should not normally exceed 0.1m/s at 25°C.

5.28   In schools for pupils with physical difficulties or profound and multiple learning difficulties or in which there may be pupils under 7 years old, or with impaired sensitivity, such as epileptic pupils, the surface temperature of any hot water radiators that might be touched should be below 43°C. Underfloor heating is considered unsuitable in special schools where a significant number of pupils are immobile and large areas of floor space are taken up with foam mats and mattresses which trap the heat. Where there are few mats and underfloor heating is preferred the surface temperature should not exceed 21°C. Supplementing the underfloor heating by other heat sources may therefore be necessary. There needs to be careful consideration as to which systems are suitable to a particular situation, as systems which draw in air from

Illustration 26
Sports: archery

floor level distribute dust, whilst those which emit warm air at or near ceiling level leave floor temperatures very low.

5.29 Stringent consideration should be given to solar gain. The thermal design, given the use of effective shading devices, should be based upon a design air temperature of 22°C, and should not allow temperatures to rise above 27°C during the school day for more than five days during the summer. Good management should ensure that shading devices are properly used, and that inactive pupils are not exposed to excessive solar radiation.

Ventilation

5.30 Because the occupation density of special schools is lower than for ordinary schools, the ventilation rates recommended in *Design Note 17*[9] of a capability of 30m³/person/hour, with 10m³/person/hour heated, for the whole building will produce ventilation rates that may not be appropriate in some spaces. In many special schools ventilation should take into account hygiene as well as comfort. In some schools, such as those for pupils with physical difficulties and those for pupils with severe (including profound and multiple) learning difficulties, ventilation rates and designs should take the risk of cross-infection into account. In

schools for such pupils teaching spaces should be able to achieve at least 2.5 air changes/hour, and in lavatory and changing areas it should be possible to achieve 10 air changes/hour. Medical inspection rooms, sick rooms and warm water play areas should also be designed with high rates of ventilation. Systems using air filters or recirculated air require careful design, and a maintenance programme is essential.

Heating load

5.31 Occupational gains are likely to be lower than in ordinary schools so that more fresh air needs to be heated, and it is desirable that this air is heated before circulation, especially in schools where the pupils may be vulnerable. These factors, as well as temperature requirements, are likely to result in higher installed heating loads and annual energy consumption values for special schools than in ordinary schools.

Drinking water

5.32 In some special schools the pupils may have difficulty in using drinking fountains. Domestic areas of the teaching accommodation should be provided with drinking water at a point where there can be cups or glasses which can be washed or may be disposable. Filtered water systems call for a maintenance commitment.

Illustration 27
Sheltered area off main recreation space

sheltered area   main play area

Warm water

5.33   All hot water delivered at outlets such as basins, sinks and showers used by the pupils should be at a temperature between 38°C and 42°C. Precautions against Legionnaires' disease must be observed and guidance is contained in the document *TM13 Minimising the risk of Legionnaires' Disease*[11].

Acoustics

5.34   The recommendations of *Design Note 17*[9] need to be supplemented, because the teaching groups envisaged are smaller in special schools than in ordinary schools. Because fewer people occupy a space of a particular size, communication distances are longer and available absorbencies are lower. Additional absorption will therefore be necessary to maintain the same reverberation periods, which should be appropriate to speech rather than music. Normal teaching rooms and associated 'quiet spaces' should have an NR* of 35. The use of carpets in teaching areas, large open spaces and circulation areas has been found beneficial in some special schools, particularly those for pupils with emotional and behavioural difficulties, in significantly reducing noise and having a positive effect on pupil behaviour.

5.35   *Design Note 25*[4] details special and different acoustic and lighting requirements for visually impaired and for hearing impaired pupils. Since it was published in 1981 there have been considerable changes in both the technical equipment available to pupils with these difficulties, and also in the special needs of the pupils. There is now generally a wider range of ability in special schools, and also an increase in the number of pupils with a dual impairment, many schools having pupils who have difficulty with both seeing and hearing. The different requirements are not intrinsically incompatible, although they have been differently illustrated in *Design Note 25* to emphasise optimum conditions for each sensory difficulty.

5.36   The residual hearing of hearing impaired pupils tends to be at frequencies at and below the 500 Hz octave band. Acoustic conditions in this area are critical, especially where powerful amplifying aids are used. Bearing in mind the probable levels of amplification, the design criteria used should be relevant to that area of the sound spectrum, with particular regard to the power levels and transmission of noise generated by plant and traffic.

Communication systems

5.37   Telephones are required for the headteacher and administrative staff, for any space set aside for specialist support services, and for any space used for staff working outside the school. An independent line to the kitchen office area may be required. In many schools the administration will be linked to the LEA's management system by computer via a phone line. The frequency of use is likely to justify an additional outside line.

5.38   In many special schools there is sometimes a need for an adult to summon help in a difficult situation. A communication system may be required linked to one or two points where help can be made rapidly available, and indicating the point from which help was summoned. Call points may be positioned in teaching areas including halls and pools, in hygiene/toilet areas, and in therapy and social spaces.

5.39   Fire alarms and fire-fighting equipment should be installed as required by the relevant authorities. Visual/audible alarms should be provided in any special school likely to have hearing impaired pupils. In schools with visually impaired pupils fire-fighting equipment, such as hose reels, extinguishers etc, should be sited so as not to intrude upon circulation routes.

5.40   Computers which are to be used for day-to-day administration should be networked. For teaching purposes they may be either stand alone, or networked.

5.41   The policy of the school will determine whether a time sound signal is necessary. Such a time sound signal can be provided in conjunction with the fire alarm system. Even where a time sound signal system is used, there should be clocks in teaching areas, to give pupils practice in telling the time and to reinforce their understanding of the concept of time.

*NR: noise rating, as defined in CIBSE Guide, volume B, section B12: Sound control.

Electrical systems

5.42   There are more items of electrical equipment per pupil in special schools than in ordinary schools. It would not be unusual during a teaching session for each child in a group to use at least one piece of equipment needing an electrical supply. In schools for pupils with physical difficulties or visual impairment there could be more. Provision of socket outlets should therefore be generous: at least four double switched outlets per space, preferably in conjunction with trunking to permit future flexibility. Furniture used should provide for cable management, thus minimising the possibility of trailing cables and facilitating the use of electrical equipment within the body of the room.

5.43   The outlets in each room should be protected by a residual current device.

5.44   Where machinery is installed that may be a hazard provision should be made for visual or audible warning, as appropriate, to indicate that it is working and for emergency stop buttons to isolate the electrical supply. The supply should be fitted with a lockable isolator or key switch.

5.45   The Health and Safety Executive publications *GS 23: Electrical safety in schools* [13] and *PM 32: The safe use of portable electrical apparatus* [14] offer safety advice on the installation of electrical equipment.

Lifts

5.46   *Design Note 18: Access for disabled people to educational buildings* [15] gives some guidance concerning suitable lifts. *BS 5588: Part 8* [16] covers additional requirements and circumstances where a lift may be an approved means of escape. This will be subject to the agreement of the local fire authority.

Safety

5.47   Safety considerations in special schools, aside from the essential provisions common to all buildings, should seek to achieve a supportive environment but without becoming overprotective. Measures can be taken to

Illustration 28
Task lighting in VI class

minimise dangers and to assist the pupils' independence and development, but it would be unrealistic to try to eliminate all risk and challenge. Supervision is an important factor in safety and the accommodation should be planned so as to facilitate this.

5.48   Safety matters to which reference is made elsewhere include:

- vehicle and pedestrian access (paras 5.3 and 5.11–5.14)

- alternative provision in some circumstances for those pupils who may have particular physical difficulties or be otherwise vulnerable (para 5.22)

- environmental considerations, including surface and water temperatures (paras 5.28 and 5.33)

- hygiene precautions, particularly in toilet and changing areas and in pools. Ball pools and soft play equipment also require strict hygiene procedures to be observed (paras 4.12, 4.18, 4.27 and 4.28)

- emergency call and intruder alarm systems (paras 4.18 and 5.38). For intruder alarms, see also *Building Bulletin 69: Crime prevention in schools: Specification, installation and maintenance of intruder alarm systems*[17]

- mechanical assistance with lifting. This is principally a health and safety matter for staff, and includes aids such as hydraulically operated changing trolleys as well as hoists (paras 4.18, 4.25 and 4.28)

- secure storage (para 4.54)

- the use of electric wheelchairs and buggies which can travel at some speed (para 5.22). This applies indoors as well as outside.

Circulation areas

5.49   The recommendations of *Design Note 18* should be adhered to, even where the school is not principally for pupils with physical difficulties. Corridor widths need to be generous: at least 1.5m, and more where there may be a significant number of pupils using wheelchairs and other mobility aids. A width greater than 2m is unlikely to be needed, unless it is associated with bays for other purposes. Obstructions, including mat wells and raised thresholds, should be avoided. Where smoke doors have to be provided at intervals along circulation spaces it is usually possible to agree with the local fire authority that these be held open by means of electromagnetic devices linked to the fire alarm system. For the visually impaired the use of colour and contrast to identify skirtings, door frames and any potentially hazardous feature such as a post or column can be helpful. Changes in texture on both horizontal and vertical surfaces can help to identify location, and surface treatment is important for the hearing impaired. Lighting, both natural and artificial, needs careful consideration. The display of pupils' work and other items needs to be considered in relation to fire safety. Further guidance is contained in *Building Bulletin 7: Fire and the design of educational buildings*[18].

5.50   Because of the increasing extent and severity of difficulty in most special school populations single-storey buildings can allow greater flexibility and convenience in use. However, this is not always possible and may not be important in the case of schools for pupils with moderate learning difficulties or emotional and behavioural difficulties without other significant disabilities. Neither need it be crucial for schools for pupils with hearing or visual difficulties.

5.51   Wherever possible the alternative of a ramp or steps should be provided between any changes in floor level; the slope of ramps should preferably not exceed 1 in 15. Handrails should be incorporated at all changes of level, as steps may be negotiated by some pupils with mobility difficulties provided a secure handrail is correctly located. Where there are pupils with visual impairment it is important to identify the nosings of stairs by means of contrasting colours. It can also be helpful to identify the top and bottom of a flight of stairs with a change in the texture of the floor finish.

Escape

5.52   *Building Bulletin 7* provides guidance on general principles of planning for escape. However, in the case of a special school certain recommendations may need to be reviewed in the light of the special needs of the pupils for which the building provides. Unassisted escape by pupils may be slower or indeed impossible, and any evacuation of the building is likely to rely heavily on the assistance of staff. Early advice must be sought and the requirements of the local fire authority complied with. An alarm system which includes flashing lights as well as an audible warning may be necessary.

5.53   Alternative means of escape should be provided. Where accommodation is at ground level direct escape from all teaching spaces can often be achieved. Staircases should include a refuge at the upper level, preferably a protected lobby, where any disabled pupil who is unable to negotiate stairs can wait in safety for assistance out of the building without impeding the escape of others. Stair lifts are not recommended for use in schools.

5.54   In some circumstances a lift may be accepted as a means of escape provided it complies with *BS 5588: Part 8* [16] and is approved by the local fire authority.

Specification of materials, finishes and fittings

5.55   Except in practical and other potentially wet areas, floors are often mostly carpeted for warmth, comfort and improved acoustics. Where vinyl or ceramic tiles are used they should have a good non-slip surface, and correct maintenance procedures must be observed if their non-slip properties are to be retained. Where walking frames and other mobility aids are used, a non-slip surface may have disadvantages, and here the alternatives will need careful consideration. Generally a balance will have to be struck between surfaces which are warm and sound-absorbing and those which are robust, easily clean-

able and hygienic. Corners may need protection.

5.56   When designing and specifying glazing, it should be remembered that pupils with special needs may be subject to additional risks because of difficulties in mobility, visual impairment, lack of awareness of their surroundings or unpredictable behaviour. Low-level windows are, however, often desirable and full-height vision panels will be necessary in many doors. These will require safety glazing. It may be advisable for all glazing in some schools to be to a higher safety specification than is generally necessary. Opening windows should not project where children might walk into them.

Equipment and furniture

5.57   For pupils with special needs particular attention must often be paid to safety measures in practical areas where machinery and other potentially hazardous equipment is provided. Some equipment may be located in a lockable materials store, while machinery may include special safety adaptations. Warning lights and buzzers may be needed. Kilns must always be suitably enclosed and well ventilated. Secure storage for hazardous substances associated with practical work and science must be provided, and any science preparation room should be lockable. The height of worktops and location of taps can affect safety. In some schools a number of height-adjustable tables and worktops may be helpful, and where scientific experiments are carried out by pupils with physical difficulties sitting at tables or benches measures, such as the provision of sunken surfaces, may need to be taken to allow for the possible spillage of dangerous substances.

6 Area requirements

Teaching spaces

6.1 Not surprisingly, experience obtained from visiting special schools over the last few years suggests that there is range of sizes of space that relates both to the range of activities that can be accommodated, and to the physical and other difficulties of the pupils. For example with general classroom accommodation a small space may be suitable only for intensive face-to-face work with a group or intensive table work with one to three pupils and an adult. A medium-size space could be used for a range of table work for a whole class group, although it would restrict the amount of practical work that could be done. But if the group contained non-ambulant pupils, their number would be restricted, even for table work. A large class base would allow a full class group to undertake the majority of general classroom activities even if it contained a high proportion of

non-ambulant pupils. Observation has made clear that, although the absolute size of a space is not critical, there are area thresholds which constrain the activities that are possible.

6.2 This has led to a 'menu' approach to assessing the area requirements of special schools. This is illustrated in Table 1. The menu shows the range of sizes of teaching space that are likely to be necessary, and relates to specified numbers and difficulties which can be accommodated for certain activities. It makes reference to the drawings elsewhere in the Bulletin of examples from the range. These include the appropriate furniture and equipment. All the possible permutations of size of space, educational activity and pupil need cannot be illustrated, but the selected examples should offer basic guidance in most cases. Table 1 is thus intended to inform the process of room size selection appro-

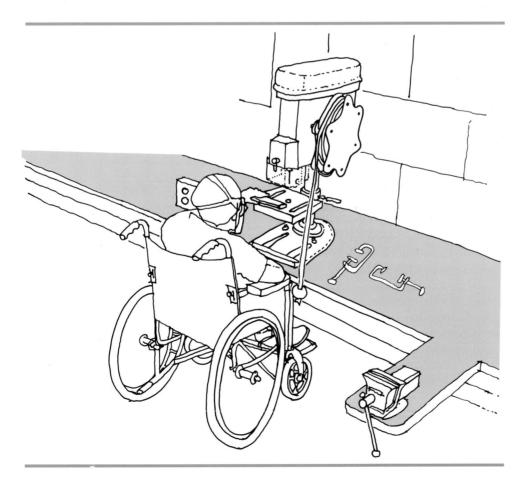

Illustration 29
**Specially adapted equipment for technology.
Pupil with limited arm movement is locating wood in place for clamping before operating adapted drill handle by means of a rope pulley.**

priate to the educational needs of any particular group of pupils. These room areas are exclusive of teaching storage.

6.3   Many LEAs are considering how best to reorganise their special school provision, and they may wish to consider converting redundant ordinary school buildings for use as special schools. The menu examples therefore reflect the range of sizes of teaching space most commonly found in existing schools. The areas shown are indicative rather than absolute figures. The shape of teaching spaces greatly affects furnishing and equipping, and should be taken into account.

6.4   Using Table 1 as a basis, schedules of teaching accommodation can be determined for a range of special schools of various types and sizes. Typical examples are illustrated in Tables 2–13. The tables are accompanied by explanatory notes. The accommodation in these schedules is intended to provide for staffing in accordance with the guidance in DES Circular 11/90[3].

6.5   A qualitative and quantitative approach has been used to the scheduling of teaching spaces. The general principle has been adopted that for pupils with special educational need the pastoral relationship is significant, and therefore a suitable class base for each organisational class group is required. In addition, the entitlement of pupils with special educational need to the National Curriculum requires that those areas of the curriculum that need specialised spaces and equipment, such as science, design technology, art, etc, are provided with separate spaces where appropriate. A basic input to the schedule of spaces is the number of teachers. Circular 11/90 requires consideration of the special educational needs for which the school is provided, and provides guidance for determining the number of teachers and special support assistants needed for a particular school; adjustments for age range are part of this guidance. Once the number of staff is known the assessment of space follows.

6.6   For primary age pupils a class base of adequate size is provided for each class teacher and teaching group. Provision is also made for practical work with

food, clay and other materials other than in the class base. Physical education is assumed to be accommodated in the hall until the number of teaching groups reaches 14. This assumes that 5% of a pupil's time might be spent on physical education indoors, giving a total load on the hall of 70% of its availability, and leaves some time for other activities to take place in the hall.

6.7   A similar but more complex procedure is followed for secondary age pupils. As with primary age pupils a class base is provided. The demand for specialist space is assessed on a curriculum percentage basis, the available teaching time being based on 80% of the time of all teachers (including the head teacher). However, the need to provide facilities for the National Curriculum leads to the provision of specialised space with low utilisation rates, and to a degree of compromise in small schools, particularly in areas such as design technology and music.

Teaching area tables

6.8   Schedules similar to those illustrated have been constructed for a range of special schools and the resultant teaching areas per pupil have been used for Tables 14–16, which show teaching area per pupil for all-age, primary and secondary schools. These tables are extended to provide not only for a range of school sizes, but also for a range of special educational needs that are divided into six categories related to the need for teaching area. They are intended to be used at feasibility stage as an indication only of the area per pupil likely to result from a detailed analysis of requirements and will always be subject to in-depth consideration of the teaching areas necessary for an individual scheme. They relate to purpose-built accommodation.

6.9   The use of the tables is self-explanatory with regard to age range and school size. Explanation of the six area categories is however necessary. There are three factors involved:

a   The staffing ratio, which affects the number and size of teaching groups, together with the number of special support assistants, which affects the number of adults who need space in teaching areas.

b The physical aspects of the particular special educational need being provided for. Clearly pupils in wheelchairs or using mobility aids need more space around them than able-bodied pupils; similarly pupils with emotional and behavioural problems need a greater degree of physical separation.

c The curriculum of the school. For example, the need in some special schools to provide a curriculum for sensory development.

6.10 The use of types of school, for example MLD or EBD, is a shorthand expression for the special educational needs of its pupils. Taking the MLD school as an example, pupils at such schools may have additional difficulties, with the learning difficulties being overlaid with physical or behavioural difficulties. In the SLD school the proportion of pupils with PMLD is variable and usually significant. Such additional difficulties directly affect staffing and the need for teaching space. Some flexibility is therefore required when the teaching area per pupil is being considered, so that regard can be given to the degree of difficulty to be dealt with in any particular case. For this reason each of the types of school indicated on the tables extends over three of the six columns.

6.11 Categories indicated on Tables 2–23 are for the four types of school for which schedules are included. For the many special schools dealing with other special educational need, for example visual or hearing impairment, or specific learning difficulty such as dyslexia, guidance can only be general. The factors affecting teaching area in 6.9 above must be taken into account. For example, the range of problems dealt with in a school for the visually impaired might be simple, uncomplicated by learning difficulty, perhaps making little use of braille, and would need a minimum staffing level, and would have a curriculum like that of an ordinary school. Another such school could be dealing with many pupils whose major problem was severe loss of vision, but who also had physical or severe learning difficulties, and needed a higher staffing level,

and with a curriculum including sensory development. Proper consideration of these issues should enable a valid guideline figure for teaching area to be established at an early stage.

6.12 The concept of 'balance area' used for assessing the area of ordinary schools is equally appropriate to special schools. Balance area is area that needs to be added to teaching area to arrive at a gross area within which a complete school can be provided. For example, in arriving at an area for ordinary primary schools a multiplier of 1.7 applied to the teaching area is often used. In deriving it for special schools consideration needs to be given to the demand for the spaces described in Chapter 4. Schedules for complete schools have been prepared, and examples are shown in Tables 17–22. As can be expected, the area that needs to be added to teaching area to produce the gross area varies in line with the size of school. All schools need to provide a number of spaces irrespective of the number of pupils, such as the head teacher's room, medical room, etc, as well as areas that do vary with pupil numbers, such as pupils' lavatories, dining space, etc. In general, because more teaching area is provided for pupils with more severe difficulties, the corresponding need for more balance area can be met as a fairly constant proportion of teaching area.

6.13 Allowance for balance area can be made from Table 23, which gives appropriate multipliers.

6.14 With regard to dining it will be clear from the schedules of complete schools that with larger schools the provision of a fully separate facility enabling the whole school to dine at one sitting will be difficult within the balance area parameter described. A degree of compromise will be required if this desirable provision is to be made within the multiplier suggested, such as use of part of the hall or other space.

6.15 No specific provision is shown in the schedules for 'case conferences' and similar activities. It is considered that enough small spaces that are not heavily used should be provided so that these activities can be absorbed.

Tables

Menu

Table 1   Menu of teaching spaces

Space type	Size (m²)	Potential range of activities	Pupils in group Primary	Pupils in group Secondary	Illustration reference
Nursery Areas					
	65	Full range of nursery activities	6 SLD + 2 PMLD 6/9 PD	N/a	
	90	Full range of nursery activities	6 SLD + 4 PMLD 9/12 PD	N/a	Fig 11
General Teaching Areas					
	36	General teaching, reference, some practical work	Too small for Primary group	8 EBD	Fig 10
	45	General teaching, quiet area, some practical work	8/10 MLD 7/8 EBD 7/8 SLD	8/10 MLD 8/9 EBD 7/8 SLD	Fig 6
	54	All teaching activities including quiet areas, bays for practical work and immediate pupil access to a wide range of resources	8/12 MLD 8 EBD 8 SLD 6 SLD + 2 PMLD 6/8 PD	10/12 MLD 8/10 EBD 8 SLD 6 SLD + 2 PMLD 6/8 PD	Fig 4
	65	All teaching activities including quiet areas, bays for practical work and immediate pupil access to a wide range of resources	6/10 PD	6/10 PD	
	72	Resource base, including space for posture aids for teaching programme	8/10 PMLD	8 PMLD	Fig 5
	90	Resource base, including space for posture aids for teaching programme	10 PMLD	10 PMLD	
Leavers' Bases					
	45	Older pupils' base for formal work		Secondary schools 8–10 pupils	
	54	Older pupils' base for formal work		Secondary schools 10–12 pupils	
	72	Post-16 base in SLD or PD school		8–12 pupils	
Specialist Teaching Areas					
Practical bay	15	Practical area for primary work	4/6 All except PD		
	25	Practical area for primary work	4 PD		
Science	25	Nucleus area used in conjunction with a classroom	N/a	4 Pupils + 4/8 in the classroom	Fig 1c
	45	Fitted and serviced space	N/a	6/7 EBD 8 MLD 6 PD	Fig 1b
	65	Fitted and serviced space to support wider range of work	N/a	8/9 EBD 10 MLD 8 PD	
Food technology	15	Bay for cooking	2/4 All except PD	N/a	

Table 1 Continued

Space type	Size (m²)	Potential range of activities	Pupils in group Primary	Secondary	Illustration reference
	25	Nucleus cooking area, used in conjunction with classroom	N/a	4 All except PD + 4/8 in classroom	
	45	Area for cooking, home studies	4/6 SLD	4/8 All	
	65	Area for cooking, food technology, home studies, social/life skills	N/a	4/8 All	
Social/Life skills	75	Area for cooking, food technology, home studies, social/life skills, plus flat/house for 16+	N/a	6/8 All	Fig 2
Design technology	45	Practical area linked with design technology area	N/a	4/6 All	
	65	Fitted out mixed material area	N/a	6/8 All	Fig 8a
	85	Fitted out mixed material area, plus design area	N/a	8/10 All	Fig 8b
Science/Technology	65	Fitted out practical area in SLD	N/a	6/8 SLD	
Art and clay	45	2-dimensional work	N/a	7/8 All	
	65	2- and 3-dimensional work	N/a	7/8 All	
Music	45	Music making, drama	Whole Group	Whole Group	
	60	Music making, drama, movement	Whole Group	Whole Group	
Physical education	140	Apparatus work and games if needed in addition to timetabled hall	Whole Group	Whole Group	

Supplementary Teaching Spaces

Space type	Size (m²)	Potential range of activities	Pupils in group Primary	Secondary	Illustration reference
Small group room	6	Withdrawal, one-to-one work	1 or 2 All	1 or 2 All	
Small group room	12	Individual or small group teaching	1 to 4 All	1 to 4 All	
Group room	20	Small group discussion and table work	3 to 6 All	3 to 6 All	
Audio-visual room	12	Light and/or sound stimulation work	1 to 2 SLD or PMLD		
	45	Television, music, drama	Whole Group	Whole Group	
Soft play	30		2 to 6 SLD or PMLD		
Warm water pool	45	For sensory development or therapy (Specialist brief necessary)	2 to 3 SLD, PMLD, or PD		Fig 17
Library	15	Bay off corridor	Minimal primary	Too small for secondary	
	25/30	Resource and study	N/a	6 All	
	45/60	Braille library	N/a	6 VI	

Communal Teaching Spaces

Space type	Size (m²)	Potential range of activities	Pupils in group Primary	Secondary	Illustration reference
Hall	120	Assembly, dining, physical education, small audience occasions	Small all-age schools and primary		Fig 15
	120	Assembly, dining, physical education, small audience occasions		Small secondary schools	
	150	Assembly, dining, physical education, small audience occasions		Large all-age and secondary schools	
Social areas	45	Older pupils' informal social education; table games, comfortable chairs, coffee		Secondary schools	

Teaching area schedules

Table 2   Teaching areas for primary school for 85 pupils with SLD

Room type	Size (m²)	Pupils in room	Number of rooms	Total pupils	Total area (m²)
Nursery/Infants *	65	8	1	8	65
Infant classroom *	45	7	2	14	90
Infant classroom *	54	8	2	16	108
Junior classroom *	54	8	5	40	270
Group room	12	0	2	0	24
Practical	15	0	1	0	15
Cooking bay	15	0	1	0	15
Library	15	0	1	0	15
Hall	120	0	1	0	120
Music	45	0	1	0	45
Light and sound	12	0	1	0	12
Soft play	30	0	1	0	30
Warm water pool	45	0	1	0	45
PMLD resource base *	65	7	1	7	65
TOTALS			21	85	919

Special support assistants (5.5:1)	15.4	
Teachers (6.2:1)	13.7	
Teaching bases	11	Teaching area per pupil 10.81

Notes

The staffing shown has been based upon DES Circular 11/90 with the assumption that about 30% of the pupils will have PMLD, with an age range from 3 to 11. As with the all-age school in Table 4 the basic organisational pattern will be class groups related to age as well as difficulty. The accommodation should offer appropriate support to Key Stages 1 and 2 of the National Curriculum, as well as to the sensory curriculum. With 11 teaching groups using the hall for indoor physical education, about 33 sessions a week, music and drama activities have been provided for in a separate space.

* Teaching bases.

Table 3   Teaching areas for secondary school for 90 pupils with SLD

Room type	Size (m²)	Pupils in room	Number of rooms	Total pupils	Total area (m²)
Senior class base *	54	8	5	40	270
Upper class base *	45	7	5	35	225
Group room	12	0	3	0	36
Library	25	0	1	0	25
Hall	150	0	1	0	150
Music	60	0	1	0	60
Food technology	65	0	1	0	65
Science/Technology	65	0	1	0	65
Art and clay	65	0	1	0	65
Post-16 base *	45	7	1	7	45
Social/Life skills	75	0	1	0	75
Light and sound	12	0	1	0	12
Warm water pool	45	0	1	0	45
PMLD resource base *	72	8	1	8	72
TOTALS			24	90	1210

Special support assistants (5.5:1)	16.3
Teachers (6.2:1)	14.5
Teaching bases	12

Teaching area per pupil 13.44

Notes

The staffing shown has been based upon DES Circular 11/90 with the assumption that about 30% of the pupils will have PMLD, with an age range from 11 to 18. The basic organisational pattern for all pupils will be related to age as well as difficulty. The size of teaching space provided should enable two or three pupils with PMLD to be integrated in the teaching groups, with the PMLD resource base used for those activities appropriate to PMLD pupils. Teaching and support staff numbers should be able to support this approach. The accommodation also reflects the entitlement of all pupils to the National Curriculum at appropriate levels. Spaces for practical activities in science, technology, and art, as well as domestic activities, have therefore been provided. For the oldest pupils, perhaps two groups in this size of school, a separate base and social/life skills area have been specified. Appropriate spaces to support the sensory curriculum are also provided. With 12 teaching groups using the hall for indoor physical education, about 33 sessions a week, music and drama activities have been provided for in a separate space.

*Teaching bases.

Table 4   Teaching areas for all-age school for 120 pupils with SLD

Room type	Size (m²)	Pupils in room	Number of rooms	Total pupils	Total area (m²)
Nursery/Infants *	65	8	1	8	65
Infant classroom *	54	8	2	16	108
Junior classroom *	54	8	4	32	216
Senior class base *	45	7	5	35	225
PMLD resource base *	72	7/8	2	15	144
Group room	12	0	2	0	24
Group room	20	0	1	0	20
Practical	15	0	1	0	15
Library	15	0	1	0	15
Hall	150	0	1	0	150
Music	45	0	1	0	45
Food technology	65	0	1	0	65
Science/Technology	65	0	1	0	65
Art and clay	65	0	1	0	65
Post-16 base *	45	7	2	14	90
Social/Life skills	75	0	1	0	75
Light and sound	12	0	1	0	12
Soft play	30	0	1	0	30
Warm water pool	45	0	1	0	45
TOTALS			30	120	1474

Special support assistants (5.5:1)	21.7	
Teachers (6.6:1)	19.8	
Teaching bases	16	Teaching area per pupil 12.28

Notes

The staffing shown has been based upon DES Circular 11/90 with the assumption that about 30% of the pupils will have profound and multiple learning difficulties (PMLD), with an age range from 3 to 18. The basic organisational pattern for all pupils will be related to age as well as difficulty. The size of teaching space provided should enable two or three pupils with PMLD to be integrated in the teaching groups, with the PMLD resource base used for those activities appropriate to PMLD pupils. Two such bases are provided, one for younger and one for older children. Teaching and support staff numbers should be able to support this approach. The accommodation also reflects the entitlement of all pupils to the National Curriculum at appropriate levels. Spaces for practical activities in science, technology, and art, as well as domestic activities, have therefore been provided for both younger and older pupils. The practical bay provided for the younger end of the school will be used for work not appropriate to the specialist spaces for older children. For the oldest pupils, a group that may have 14 to 18 pupils, separate bases and a social/life skills area have been specified. Appropriate spaces to support the sensory curriculum are also provided.

*Teaching bases.

Table 5   Teaching areas for primary school for 50 pupils with MLD

Room type	Size (m²)	Pupils in room	Number of rooms	Total pupils	Total area (m²)
Infant classroom *	54	10	2	20	108
Junior classroom *	45	10	3	30	135
Group room	12	0	2	0	24
Practical	15	0	1	0	15
Cooking bay	15	0	1	0	15
Library	15	0	1	0	15
Hall	120	0	1	0	120
TOTALS			11	50	432

Special support assistants (10.0:1)	5.0	
Teachers (9.3:1)	5.4	
Teaching bases	5	Teaching area per pupil 8.64

Notes
The staffing shown, based upon the least degree of difficulty suggested in DES Circular 11/90, has led to a choice of basic class groups of 10. As with the small EBD primary school, the assumption is that the school is being provided to support the early identification of children with this specific educational need, with the objective of returning them to mainstream as soon as appropriate. No particular age skew is anticipated and the basic organisational pattern will follow that of a mainstream primary school. Staff numbers support this approach. The accommodation should be able to support all the National Curriculum at all levels for Key Stages 1 and 2. Facilities have therefore been provided in separate supplementary areas for practical work of making and modelling including clay work, and for work with food. The timetabled use of the hall for physical education will not be high, and should allow this multi-use space to be available for some music and drama.

*Teaching bases

Table 6   Teaching areas for secondary school for 120 pupils with MLD

Room type	Size (m²)	Pupils in room	Number of rooms	Total pupils	Total area (m²)
Lower classroom *	45	10	2	20	90
Lower classroom *	54	12	2	24	108
Upper classroom *	45	10	3	30	135
Upper classroom *	54	11	2	22	108
Group room	12	0	2	0	24
Science room	65	0	2	0	130
Food technology	65	0	1	0	65
Design technology	65	0	1	0	65
Art and clay	65	0	1	0	65
Music	45	0	1	0	45
Library	25	0	1	0	25
Hall	150	0	1	0	150
Social	45	0	1	0	45
Leavers' base *	54	12	2	24	108
TOTALS			22	120	1163

Special support assistants (20:1)	6.0	
Teachers (9.3:1)	13.0	
Teaching bases	11	Teaching area per pupil 9.69

Notes

In this case staffing, calculated on the guidance in DES Circular 11/90, has led to the choice of basic class groups of 10 to 12. Unlike the EBD secondary school the underlying assumption is that this school is unlikely to return many pupils to mainstream, although that may be a guiding objective. It is also expected that there will be a skew towards older pupils as those with difficulties become less able to keep up with the pace of ordinary schools. The basic organisational pattern follows that of an ordinary secondary school and it is a principle that the accommodation should support pupils' entitlement to the National Curriculum at Key Stages 3 and 4. Science, if taking 15% of curriculum time in full class groups (i.e. 11 groups), will require two spaces. With an average teaching group size of 11.6 the frequency of use of the teaching spaces, i.e. excluding group rooms, social, and library, is 61%. In view of the number of leavers (a minimum year group of 24), two bases supplemented by a social area have been provided for them, and this should permit the design of a differentiated adult environment for this older age group.

*Teaching bases.

Table 7   Teaching areas for all-age school for 100 pupils with MLD

Room type	Size (m²)	Pupils in room	Number of rooms	Total pupils	Total area (m²)
Infant classroom *	54	11	2	22	108
Infant classroom *	54	12	2	24	108
Lower class base *	54	12	2	24	108
Upper class base *	45	10	2	20	90
Group room	12	0	2	0	24
Group room	20	0	1	0	20
Practical bay	15	0	1	0	15
Science room	65	0	1	0	65
Food technology	65	0	1	0	65
Design technology	65	0	1	0	65
Art and clay	45	0	1	0	45
Music	45	0	1	0	45
Library	25	0	1	0	25
Hall	150	0	1	0	150
Social	45	0	1	0	45
Leavers' base *	45	10	1	10	45
TOTALS			21	100	1023

Special support assistants (13.3:1)	7.5
Teachers (9.2:1)	10.9
Teaching bases	9

Teaching area per pupil 10.23

Notes

The staffing shown has been based upon the guidance in DES Circular 11/90, and has led to a choice of basic class groups of 10 to 12. It was also expected that this all-age MLD school would have an age profile skewed towards older pupils, so that there would be at least five class groups of secondary age working on Key Stages 3 and 4 of the National Curriculum. Class groups would form the basic organisational pattern for the younger pupils and for tutorial purposes, but, as for other all-age schools, the facility to work in smaller groups related to age and ability in the secondary age band was considered to be desirable in order to maintain the opportunity for return to mainstream. Staff numbers should be able to support this approach, but the accommodation should be also able to support the National Curriculum at appropriate levels. Specialist spaces for science, design technology, and art have therefore been provided. The overall frequency of use of the 15 teaching spaces, i.e. excluding the group rooms, social area and the library, will be about 57% of the available time. The average teaching group size will be about 11.5. Secondary age pupils may need to work in smaller groups in some specialist areas which implies that other spaces will have to accommodate larger groups, perhaps up to 16, and this has been considered in briefing. A practical bay has been provided for the younger end of the school because the specialist spaces for older children would not be appropriate. One of the class bases has been identified as a leavers' base to underpin the sense of progression. The numbers also allow a social area to be considered.

The frequency of use of 57% is low, but is a consequence of providing tutorial bases for each class in the form of classrooms, and providing space to support the specialist aspects of the curriculum. A building to this brief would be able to support more intensive staffing appropriate to more complex difficulties than simple learning difficulty. If 13 teachers were deployed the average size of teaching group would be reduced to say 9.8, allowing more work in small groups, and the spaces would be used more economically, the frequency of use rising to 68%.

*Teaching bases.

Table 8   Teaching areas for primary school for 50 pupils with EBD

Room type	Size (m²)	Pupils in room	Number of rooms	Total pupils	Total area (m²)
Infant classroom *	54	7	3	21	162
Junior classroom *	45	7	3	21	135
Junior classroom *	54	8	1	8	54
Group room	12	0	2	0	24
Practical bay	15	0	1	0	15
Cooking bay	15	0	1	0	15
Library	15	0	1	0	15
Hall	120	0	1	0	120
TOTALS			13	50	540

Special support assistants (6.7:1)	7.5	
Teachers (6.0:1)	8	
Teaching bases	7	Teaching area per pupil 10.80

Notes
Staffing calculated on the guidance in DES Circular 11/90 has led to a choice of basic class groups of seven or eight. The assumption is that a primary special school is being provided to support the early identification of children with this specific educational need, with the objective of returning them to mainstream as soon as appropriate. No particular age skew is anticipated. The basic organisational pattern will follow that of a one form entry mainstream primary school and staff numbers support this approach. The accommodation should be able to support all the National Curriculum at all levels for Key Stages 1 and 2. Facilities have therefore been provided in the form of separate supplementary areas for practical work of making and modelling including clay work, and for work with food. The timetabled use for the hall for physical education will not be high, and should allow this multi-use space to be available for some music and drama.

*Teaching bases.

Table 9   Teaching areas for secondary school for 60 pupils with EBD

Room type	Size (m²)	Pupils in room	Number of rooms	Total pupils	Total area (m²)
Lower classroom *	36	7	3	21	108
Upper classroom *	36	7	1	7	36
Upper classroom *	45	8	3	24	135
Group room	12	0	2	0	24
Science nucleus	25	0	1	0	25
Science room	65	0	1	0	65
Food technology	45	0	1	0	45
Design technology	65	0	1	0	65
Art and clay	65	0	1	0	65
Library	25	0	1	0	25
Hall	120	0	1	0	120
Social	45	0	1	0	45
Leavers' base *	45	8	1	8	45
TOTALS			18	60	803

Special support assistants (6.7:1)	9.0	
Teachers (6.2:1)	9.7	
Teaching bases	8	Teaching area per pupil 13.38

Notes

In this case staffing calculated on the recommendations of DES Circular 11/90 has led to the choice of basic class groups of seven or eight. The assumption is that this 11 to 16 school supplements special provision for primary age pupils, and shares the same approach of early identification and return to mainstream as soon as appropriate. Nevertheless a skew towards older pupils may occur because of the problem of return late in school life. The basic organisational pattern follows that of an ordinary secondary school. The accommodation is required to support the National Curriculum at all levels for Key Stages 3 and 4. Science, if taking 15% of curriculum time in full class groups, will require more than one space, so that in addition to a laboratory, a science nucleus sited between two classrooms has been specified to enable two groups to be timetabled at one time. The timetabled use of the hall for physical education will not be high, and should allow this multi-use space to be available for other activities. The balance of teaching spaces provided, i.e. seven classrooms and six specialist areas, reflects a fairly normal curriculum balance with more than 50% of time spent in general classrooms and less than 50% in specialist areas. With an average teaching group size of 7.5 the13 teaching spaces, i.e. excluding group rooms, social, library, and the science nucleus which is a substitute use, the frequency of use of space is about 60% of the available time. As for the all-age school one of the rooms has been identified as a leavers' base so that the accommodation can underpin a sense of progression, and in view of their numbers (a minimum year group of 12) has been supplemented by a social area.

*Teaching bases.

Table 10 Teaching area for all-age school for 60 pupils with EBD

Room type	Size (m²)	Pupils in room	Number of rooms	Total pupils	Total area (m²)
Junior classroom *	54	7	1	7	54
Lower classroom *	45	7	2	14	90
Upper classroom *	36	7	1	7	36
Upper classroom *	45	8	3	24	135
Group room	12	0	2	0	24
Science room	45	0	1	0	45
Food technology	45	0	1	0	45
Design technology	65	0	1	0	65
Art and clay	65	0	1	0	65
Library	30	0	1	0	30
Hall	120	0	1	0	120
Leavers' base *	54	8	1	8	54
TOTALS			16	60	763

Special support assistants (6.7:1) 9.0
Teachers (6.0:1) 10.0
Teaching bases 8   Teaching area per pupil 12.72

Notes
Staffing calculated on the guidance in DES Circular 11/90 has led to a choice of basic class groups of seven or eight. It is expected that this all-age EBD school will have an age profile skewed towards older pupils, so that there will be at least four class groups of secondary age working on Key Stages 3 and 4 of the National Curriculum. Class groups would form the basic organisational pattern for the younger pupils and for tutorial purposes, but the facility to work in smaller groups related to age and ability in the secondary age band was considered to be desirable for these pupils to maintain the opportunity for return to mainstream. Staff numbers should be able to support this approach. The corollary is that the accommodation should be able to support all the National Curriculum at all levels. Specialist spaces for science, design technology, and art have therefore been provided. With this number of staff the overall frequency of use of the teaching spaces, i.e. excluding the group rooms and the library, will be in excess of 60% with an average teaching group of fewer than seven pupils. One of the class bases has been identified as a leavers' base to underpin the sense of progression by the accommodation. This frequency of use is to be expected in the small all-age school providing for all areas of the National Curriculum.

*Teaching bases.

Table 11 Teaching areas for primary school for 60 pupils with PD

Room type	Size (m²)	Pupils in room	Number of rooms	Total pupils	Total area (m²)
Nursery/Infants *	65	7	1	7	65
Infant classroom *	54	7	2	14	108
Infant/Junior *	54	8	1	8	54
Junior classroom *	54	7	1	7	54
Junior classroom *	54	8	3	24	162
Group room	20	0	2	0	40
Practical	25	0	1	0	25
Cooking bay	25	0	1	0	25
Music/audio-visual	45	0	1	0	45
Library	25	0	1	0	25
Hall	120	0	1	0	120
TOTALS			15	60	723

Special support assistants (5.0:1)	12.0
Teachers (6.2:1)	9.6
Teaching bases	8

Teaching area per pupil 12.05

Notes
Staffing calculated on the recommendations of DES Circular 11/90 has led to a choice of basic class groups of seven or eight. As with other small primary special schools, the basic organisational pattern will follow that of a mainstream primary school. The accommodation should be able to support the National Curriculum at all levels for Key Stages 1 and 2. Facilities have therefore been provided in separate supplementary areas for practical work in making and modelling, including clay work, and for work with food. Larger area standards have been selected to provide access.

* Teaching bases.

Table 12   Teaching areas for secondary school for 90 pupils with PD

Room type	Size (m²)	Pupils in room	Number of rooms	Total pupils	Total area (m²)
Lower class base *	54	8	2	16	108
Lower class base *	54	7	3	21	162
Upper class base *	54	8	3	24	162
Upper class base *	54	7	3	21	162
Group room	20	0	2	0	40
Science room	65	0	2	0	130
Food technology	65	0	1	0	65
Design technology	65	0	1	0	65
Art and clay	65	0	1	0	65
Music	45	0	1	0	45
Library	30	0	1	0	30
Hall	120	0	1	0	120
Warm water pool	45	0	1	0	45
Post-16*	72	8	1	8	72
TOTALS			23	90	1271

Special support assistants (5.5:1)	18.0	
Teachers (6.0:1)	15.0	
Teaching bases	12	Teaching area per pupil 14.12

Notes

This small special school benefits from the additional staff provided for the post-16 pupils. Nevertheless the pastoral organisation has been assumed to be class groups of seven or eight pupils throughout. The basic organisational pattern follows that of an ordinary secondary school and it is a principle that the accommodation should support pupils' entitlement to all levels of the National Curriculum at Key Stages 3 and 4. Science, if taking 15% of curriculum time in full class groups, will require two spaces which may be used for 90% of the time. The timetabled use of the hall for physical education at 5% of time will be 60%, and will leave some availability for other activities. Overall frequency of use of the 19 teaching spaces, excluding group rooms, library and warm water pool, will be 63%.

* Teaching bases.

Table 13 Teaching areas for all-age school for 100 pupils with PD

Room type	Size (m²)	Pupils in room	Number of rooms	Total pupils	Total area (m²)
Nursery/Infants *	65	8	1	8	65
Infant classroom *	54	7	4	28	216
Lower class base *	54	7	4	28	216
Upper class base *	54	7	4	28	216
Group room	20	0	2	0	40
Practical bay	25	0	1	0	25
Science room	65	0	1	0	65
Food technology	65	0	1	0	65
Design technology	65	0	1	0	65
Art and clay	65	0	1	0	65
Music	45	0	1	0	45
Library	25	0	1	0	25
Hall	150	0	1	0	150
Warm water pool	45	0	1	0	45
Post-16 *	54	8	1	8	54
TOTALS			25	100	1357

Special support assistants (5.0:1)	20.0	
Teachers (6.1:1)	16.4	
Teaching bases	14	Teaching area per pupil 13.57

Notes
Staffing calculated on the recommendations of DES Circular 11/90 has led to a choice of a basic class size of about seven. As for other all-age schools the work of younger pupils will be class based primary mode. For secondary age pupils facilities are provided to enable working in smaller groups that can be age and ability related. In a school of this size there are likely to be about 40 secondary age pupils. The five or six classrooms they will use are anticipated to develop subject specialisms as well as having a pastoral function. There are also spaces for science, design technology, and art. The overall frequency of use of the 20 teaching spaces, i.e. excluding the group rooms, practical bay, library, and warm water pool, will be in excess of 65%. There should be time for the younger pupils to have use of the music, art and other spaces. If each class group uses the hall for indoor physical education for 5% of the time, the aggregate will load the space for 70% of the time, leaving little available for other activities.

* Teaching bases.

Guideline teaching areas

Table 14 The most commonly found sizes of primary special schools and teaching areas required to support the curriculum

Number of pupils	Area (m²) appropriate to special educational need						
20	10.6	11.8	13.0	14.2	15.4	16.6	17.8
25	9.2	10.3	11.3	12.4	13.4	14.5	15.5
30	8.6	9.6	10.6	11.6	12.6	13.5	14.5
35	8.2	9.2	10.1	11.1	12.0	12.9	13.9
40	8.0	8.9	9.8	10.7	11.6	12.5	13.4
45	7.8	8.6	9.5	10.4	11.3	12.2	13.0
50	7.6	8.4	9.3	10.2	11.0	11.9	12.7
55	7.4	8.3	9.1	10.0	10.8	11.6	12.5
60	7.3	8.1	9.0	9.8	10.6	11.4	12.3
65	7.2	8.0	8.8	9.6	10.5	11.3	12.1
70	7.1	7.9	8.7	9.5	10.3	11.1	11.9
75	7.0	7.8	8.6	9.4	10.2	11.0	11.8
80	6.9	7.7	8.5	9.3	10.1	10.9	11.6
85	6.8	7.6	8.4	9.2	10.0	10.7	11.5
90	6.8	7.5	8.3	9.1	9.9	10.6	11.4
95	6.7	7.5	8.2	9.0	9.8	10.5	11.3
100	6.7	7.4	8.2	8.9	9.7	10.4	11.2
105	6.6	7.4	8.1	8.9	9.6	10.4	11.1
110	6.6	7.3	8.0	8.8	9.5	10.3	11.0
115	6.5	7.2	8.0	8.7	9.5	10.2	10.9
120	6.5	7.2	7.9	8.7	9.4	10.1	10.9
125	6.4	7.1	7.9	8.6	9.3	10.1	10.8
130	6.4	7.1	7.8	8.6	9.3	10.0	10.7
135	6.3	7.1	7.8	8.5	9.2	9.9	10.7
140	6.3	7.0	7.7	8.5	9.2	9.9	10.6
145	6.3	7.0	7.7	8.4	9.1	9.8	10.5
150	6.2	6.9	7.7	8.4	9.1	9.8	10.5

— — — — Range for SLD Schools

– — – — – Range for MLD Schools

———— Range for EBD Schools

·············· Range for PD Schools

Table 15   The most commonly found sizes of secondary special schools and teaching areas required to support the curriculum

Number of pupils	Area (m²) appropriate to special educational need						
30	11.0	12.1	13.2	14.3	15.4	16.5	17.6
35	10.6	11.7	12.8	13.8	14.9	16.0	17.0
40	10.4	11.4	12.5	13.5	14.5	15.6	16.6
45	10.2	11.2	12.2	13.2	14.2	15.3	16.3
50	10.0	11.0	12.0	13.0	14.0	15.0	16.0
55	9.9	10.9	11.9	12.8	13.8	14.8	15.8
60	9.8	10.7	11.7	12.7	13.7	14.6	15.6
65	9.7	10.6	11.6	12.6	13.5	14.5	15.5
70	9.6	10.5	11.5	12.4	13.4	14.4	15.3
75	9.5	10.4	11.4	12.3	13.3	14.2	15.2
80	9.4	10.4	11.3	12.2	13.2	14.1	15.1
85	9.4	10.3	11.2	12.2	13.1	14.0	15.0
90	9.3	10.2	11.2	12.1	13.0	13.9	14.9
95	9.2	10.2	11.1	12.0	12.9	13.9	14.8
100	9.2	10.1	11.0	11.9	12.9	13.8	14.7
110	9.1	10.0	10.9	11.8	12.7	13.6	14.5
120	9.0	9.9	10.8	11.7	12.6	13.5	14.4
130	8.9	9.8	10.7	11.6	12.5	13.4	14.3
140	8.9	9.7	10.6	11.5	12.4	13.3	14.2
150	8.8	9.7	10.5	11.4	12.3	13.2	14.1
160	8.7	9.6	10.5	11.4	12.2	13.1	14.0
170	8.7	9.5	10.4	11.3	12.1	13.0	13.9
180	8.6	9.5	10.4	11.2	12.1	12.9	13.8
190	8.6	9.4	10.3	11.2	12.0	12.9	13.7
200	8.5	9.4	10.2	11.1	12.0	12.8	13.7
210	8.5	9.3	10.2	11.0	11.9	12.7	13.6
220	8.5	9.3	10.1	11.0	11.8	12.7	13.5
230	8.4	9.3	10.1	10.9	11.8	12.6	13.5
240	8.4	9.2	10.1	10.9	11.7	12.6	13.4
250	8.4	9.2	10.0	10.9	11.7	12.5	13.4
260	8.3	9.1	10.0	10.8	11.6	12.5	13.3
270	8.3	9.1	9.9	10.8	11.6	12.4	13.3
280	8.3	9.1	9.9	10.7	11.6	12.4	13.2
290	8.2	9.1	9.9	10.7	11.5	12.3	13.2
300	8.2	9.0	9.8	10.7	11.5	12.3	13.1

— — — — Range for SLD Schools

·— ·— ·— Range for MLD Schools

———— Range for EBD Schools

············· Range for PD Schools

Table 16   The most commonly found sizes of all-age special schools and teaching areas required to support the curriculum

Number of pupils	Area (m²) appropriate to special educational need						
20	12.3	13.5	14.7	15.9	17.2	18.4	19.6
25	10.9	12.0	13.1	14.2	15.2	16.3	17.4
30	10.3	11.4	12.4	13.4	14.5	15.5	16.6
35	10.0	11.0	12.0	13.0	14.0	15.0	16.0
40	9.8	10.7	11.7	12.7	13.7	14.6	15.6
45	9.6	10.5	11.5	12.5	13.4	14.4	15.3
50	9.4	10.4	11.3	12.3	13.2	14.1	15.1
55	9.3	10.2	11.2	12.1	13.0	13.9	14.9
60	9.2	10.1	11.0	11.9	12.9	13.8	14.7
65	9.1	10.0	10.9	11.8	12.7	13.6	14.5
70	9.0	9.9	10.8	11.7	12.6	13.5	14.4
75	8.9	9.8	10.7	11.6	12.5	13.4	14.3
80	8.9	9.7	10.6	11.5	12.4	13.3	14.2
85	8.8	9.7	10.5	11.4	12.3	13.2	14.1
90	8.7	9.6	10.5	11.3	12.2	13.1	14.0
95	8.7	9.5	10.4	11.3	12.1	13.0	13.9
100	8.6	9.5	10.3	11.2	12.1	12.9	13.8
110	8.5	9.4	10.2	11.1	11.9	12.8	13.6
120	8.4	9.3	10.1	11.0	11.8	12.7	13.5
130	8.4	9.2	10.0	10.9	11.7	12.6	13.4
140	8.3	9.1	10.0	10.8	11.6	12.4	13.3
150	8.2	9.1	9.9	10.7	11.5	12.4	13.2
160	8.2	9.0	9.8	10.6	11.5	12.3	13.1
170	8.1	8.9	9.8	10.6	11.4	12.2	13.0
180	8.1	8.9	9.7	10.5	11.3	12.1	12.9
190	8.0	8.8	9.6	10.4	11.2	12.1	12.9
200	8.0	8.8	9.6	10.4	11.2	12.0	12.8
210	7.9	8.7	9.5	10.3	11.1	11.9	12.7
220	7.9	8.7	9.5	10.3	11.1	11.9	12.7
230	7.9	8.7	9.5	10.2	11.0	11.8	12.6
240	7.8	8.6	9.4	10.2	11.0	11.8	12.5

— — — —   Range for SLD Schools

— · — · —   Range for MLD Schools

————   Range for EBD Schools

················   Range for PD Schools

Table 17 Primary school for 60 pupils with SLD

Room type	Room size (m²)	Number of rooms	Teaching area (m²)	Gross area (m²)
Nursery/Infants	65	1	65	65
Infant classroom	45	3	135	135
Junior classroom	54	3	162	162
PMLD resource base	65	1	65	65
Group room	12	2	24	24
Teaching storage 12.5%				56
Practical bay	15	1	15	15
Cooking bay	15	1	15	15
Teaching storage 20%				6
Light and sound	12	1	12	12
Warm water pool	45	1	45	45
Teaching storage 10%				6
Soft play	30	1	30	30
Library	15	1	15	15
Hall	120	1	120	120
Teaching storage 15%				18
Staff accommodation				
Head				12
Deputy				9
Staff room				32
Parents' room				15
Secretary and reprographics				12
Staff lavatories: 3 WCs and washhand basins,				
1 shower				10
Central store				13
Medical and therapy accommodation				
Physiotherapy and store				20
Other therapists' base				8
Educational Psychologist/Interview				8
Medical Inspection room				14
Pupils' lavatories and cloaks				
10 sanitary fittings and washhand basins				65
Hygiene areas, 2 at 15m²				30
Cloaks, pool changing, etc, for 60 pupils				35
Hygiene storage				6
Wheelchair and appliance storage				10
Kitchen/Dining for 60				149
Caretaker and store				12
Plant including pool, electrics and cleaners, 3.5%				55
Circulation, partitions, etc, 17.5%				289
TOTALS			703	1593

Percentage teaching area	44.1 %
Teaching area per pupil	11.72 m²
Teaching storage as % of teaching	12.2 %
Gross area per pupil	26.55 m²

Table 18   Secondary school for 60 pupils with SLD

Room type	Room size (m²)	Number of rooms	Teaching area (m²)	Gross area (m²)
Senior class base	54	3	162	162
Upper class base	45	3	135	135
Post-16	45	1	45	45
Social/Life skills	75	1	75	75
PMLD resource base	72	1	72	72
Group room	12	2	24	24
Teaching storage 12.5%				64
Food technology	65	1	65	65
Science/Technology	65	1	65	65
Art and clay	45	1	45	45
Teaching storage 20%				35
Light and sound	12	1	12	12
Teaching storage 10%				1
Library	15	1	15	15
Hall	120	1	120	120
Teaching storage 15%				18
Staff accommodation				
Head				12
Deputy				9
Staff room				32
Parents' room				15
Secretary and reprographics				12
Staff lavatories: 3 WCs and washhand basins,				
1 shower				10
Central store				13
Medical and therapy accommodation				
Physiotherapy and store				20
Other therapists' base				8
Educational Psychologist/Interview				8
Medical Inspection room				14
Pupils' lavatories and cloaks				
10 sanitary fittings and washhand basins				65
Hygiene areas, 1 at 15m²				15
Cloaks, changing, etc, for 60 pupils				50
Hygiene storage				6
Wheelchair and appliance storage				10
Kitchen/Dining for 60				149
Caretaker and store				12
Plant including pool, electrics and cleaners, 3.5%				63
Circulation, partitions, etc, 17.5%				327
TOTALS			835	1803

Percentage teaching area	46.3%
Teaching area per pupil	13.92m²
Teaching storage as % of teaching	14.1%
Gross area per pupil	30.05m²

Table 19   Secondary school for 80 pupils with MLD

Room type	Room size (m²)	Number of rooms	Teaching area (m²)	Gross area (m²)
Lower class base	45	2	90	90
Lower class base	54	1	54	54
Upper class base	45	4	180	180
Leavers' base	54	1	54	54
Group room	12	2	24	24
Teaching storage 10%				40
Science room	65	1	65	65
Food technology	65	1	65	65
Design technology	65	1	65	65
Art and clay	45	1	45	45
Teaching storage 20%				48
Social	45	1	45	45
Library	25	1	25	25
Hall	150	1	150	150
Teaching storage 15%				23
Staff and administration				
Head				12
Deputy				9
Staff room				19
Staff work room				9
Secretary and reprographics				12
Staff lavatories: 3 WCs and washhand basins,				
1 shower				10
Central store				14
Medical and therapy accommodation				
Speech therapy				10
Psychologist/Interview, etc				8
Medical Inspection room				12
Pupils' lavatories and cloaks				
8 sanitary fittings and washhand basins				40
Cloaks, etc, for 80 pupils				20
PE Changing, boys and girls				38
Kitchen/Dining for 80 *				121
Caretaker and store				15
Plant including electrics and cleaners, 2.5%				41
Circulation, partitions, etc, 17.5%				289
TOTALS			862	1652
Percentage teaching area	52.2%			
Teaching area per pupil	10.78m²			
Teaching storage as % of teaching	12.9%			
Gross area per pupil	20.65m²			

*The area here assumes dining either in two sittings or one sitting using in addition the hall and associated circulation.

Table 20   All-age school for 160 pupils with MLD

Room type	Room size (m²)	Number of rooms	Teaching area (m²)	Gross area (m²)
Infant/Junior classroom	54	4	216	216
Lower class base	45	5	225	225
Upper class base	45	5	225	225
Leavers' base	45	2	90	90
Group room	12	2	24	24
Group room	20	1	20	20
Teaching storage 10%				78
Practical bay	15	1	15	15
Science room	65	1	65	65
Food technology	65	1	65	65
Design technology	65	1	65	65
Art and clay	65	1	65	65
Music	45	1	45	45
Teaching storage 20%				64
Social	45	1	45	45
Library	30	1	30	30
Hall	150	1	150	150
Teaching storage 15%				23
Staff accommodation				
Head				12
Deputy				9
Staff room				44
Secretary and reprographics				15
Staff lavatories: 4 WCs and washhand basins,				
2 showers				15
Central store				18
Medical and therapy accommodation				
Speech therapy				10
Psychologist/Interview, etc				8
Medical Inspection room				12
Pupils' lavatories and cloaks				
16 sanitary fittings and washhand basins				80
Cloaks, etc, for 160 pupils				40
PE Changing, boys and girls				38
Kitchen/Dining for 160 *				187
Caretaker and store				15
Plant including electrics and cleaners, 2.5%				56
Circulation, partitions, etc, 17.5%				405
TOTALS			1345	2474
Percentage teaching area	54.4%			
Teaching area per pupil	8.41m²			
Teaching storage as % of teaching	12.3%			
Gross area per pupil	15.46m²			

*The area here assumes dining either in two sittings or one sitting using in addition the hall associated circulation.

Table 21   All-age school for 45 pupils with EBD

Room type	Room size (m²)	Number of rooms	Teaching area (m²)	Gross area (m²)
Junior class base	54	1	54	54
Lower class base	45	1	45	45
Upper class base	36	2	72	72
Upper class base	45	1	45	45
Leavers' base	45	1	45	45
Group room	12	2	24	24
Teaching storage 10%				29
Science room	45	1	45	45
Food technology	45	1	45	45
Design technology	65	1	65	65
Art and clay	45	1	45	45
Teaching storage 20%				40
Library	25	1	25	25
Hall	120	1	120	120
Teaching storage 15%				18
Staff accommodation				
Head				12
Deputy				9
Staff room				21
Secretary and reprographics				12
Staff lavatories: 3 WCs and washhand basins,				
1 shower				10
Central store				12
Medical and therapy accommodation				
Educational Psychologist/Interview				8
Medical Inspection room				12
Pupils' lavatories and cloaks				
6 sanitary fittings and washhand basins				30
Cloaks, etc, for 45 pupils				11
PE Changing, boys and girls				25
Kitchen/Dining for 45				128
Caretaker and store				12
Plant including electrics and cleaners, 2.5%				32
Circulation, partitions, etc, 17.5%				223
TOTALS			630	1274
Percentage teaching area	49.5%			
Teaching area per pupil	14.00m²			
Teaching storage as % of teaching	13.8%			
Gross area per pupil	28.31m²			

Table 22　Primary school for 45 pupils with PD

Room type	Room size (m²)	Number of rooms	Teaching area (m²)	Gross area (m²)
Nursery/Infants classroom	65	1	65	65
Infant classrooom	54	2	108	108
Junior classroom	54	3	162	162
Group room	20	1	20	20
Teaching storage 12.5%				44
Practical bay	25	1	25	25
Cooking bay	25	1	25	25
Teaching storage 20%				10
Library	25	1	25	25
Hall	120	1	120	120
Teaching storage 15%				18
Staff and administration				
Head				12
Deputy				9
Staff room				24
Secretary and reprographics				12
Staff lavatories: 4 WCs and washhand basins,				
2 showers				15
Central store				12
Medical and therapy accommodation				
Physiotherapy and store				20
Other therapists/Interview				10
Medical Inspection room and treatment				18
Pupils' lavatories and cloaks				
Hygiene areas, 2 at 15m²				30
6 sanitary fittings and washhand basins				39
Cloaks, etc, for 45 pupils				11
Hygiene storage				8
Wheelchair and appliance storage				16
Kitchen/Dining for 45				128
Caretaker and store				15
Plant including electrics and cleaners, 2.5%				32
Circulation, partitions, etc, 20%				258
TOTALS			550	1291
Percentage teaching area	42.6%			
Teaching area per pupil	12.22m²			
Teaching storage as % of teaching	13.1%			
Gross area per pupil	28.69m²			

Gross area

Table 23   Gross area as a multiple of teaching area

Number of pupils	Type of school			
	SLD	MLD	EBD	PD
40	2.20		2.00	2.20
60	2.15	1.95	1.95	2.15
80	2.15	1.90	1.90	2.10
100	2.05	1.85	1.85	2.05
120	2.00	1.80		2.00
140	1.95	1.80		
160		1.75		
200		1.75		

Glossary

Audio-visual: Equipment or space used for teaching using cassette recorder, radio, television, film, etc.

Ball pool: A tank filled with plastic balls; offers support similar to a water-filled pool.

Conductive education: An holistic method of teaching based upon the acquisition and improvement of physical skills where these are severely impaired.

Sensory curriculum: That part of the curriculum of a special school designed to develop sensory responses where these are at a low level.

Soft play: Space or equipment designed to give opportunities for physical movement with minimum risk of accidental injury.

Statement: The agreed description of the special educational needs of a pupil and the resources required, given in accordance with Section 78(1) of the Education Act 1981.

Stoma care: Technical term for the procedures pertaining to bowel function where this has been interrupted by surgery.

References

1   *Special Educational Needs: Report of the Committee of Enquiry into the Education of Handicapped Children and Young People* ('Warnock Report'). Command 7212. ISBN 0 10 172120 X. HMSO, 1978.

2   *Building Bulletin 61: Designing for children with special educational needs: Ordinary schools* ISBN 0 11 270313 5. HMSO, 1984.

3   DES Circular 11/90: 'Staffing for pupils with special educational needs'. 13 December 1990.

4   *Design Note 25: Lighting and acoustic criteria for the visually handicapped and hearing impaired in schools* ISSN 0 141-2825. DES, 1981.

5   *Design Note 10: Designing for the severely handicapped* ISSN 0 141-2825. DES, 1972.

6   *Building Bulletin 71: The Outdoor Classroom* ISBN 0 11 270730 0. HMSO, 1990.

7   *Building Bulletin 67: Crime prevention in schools: Practical guidance* ISBN 0 11 270637 1. HMSO, 1987.

8   *Playground Safety Guidelines* ISBN 0 85522 405 3. DES and National Children's Play and Recreation Unit, 1992.

9   *Design Note 17: Guidelines for environmental design and fuel conservation in educational buildings* ISSN 0 141-2825. DES, 1981.

10 *CIBSE Guide,* section A1: Environmental criteria for design. ISBN 0 900953 29 2. Chartered Institute of Building Services Engineers, 1986.

11 *TM13: Minimising the risk of Legionnaires' Disease* ISBN 0 900953 34 9. Chartered Institute of Building Services Engineers, 1987.

12 *CIBSE Guide,* volume B: *Installation and equipment data,* section B12: Sound control. ISBN 0 900953 30 6. Chartered Institute of Building Services Engineers, 1986.

13 *GS 23: Electrical safety in schools* (Electricity at Work Regulations 1989). ISBN 0 11 885426 7. Health and Safety Executive, 1990.

14 *PM 32: The safe use of portable electrical apparatus* (electrical safety). ISBN 0 11 885590 5. Health and Safety Executive, 1990.

15 *Design Note 18: Access for disabled people to educational buildings,* second edition. ISSN 0 141-2825. DES, 1984.

16 *BS 5588: Fire precautions in the design and construction of buildings.* Part 8: Code of practice for means of escape for disabled people. ISBN 0 580 16408 X. British Standards Institute, 1988.

17 *Building Bulletin 69: Crime prevention in schools: Specification, installation and maintenance of intruder alarm systems* ISBN 0 11 270677 0. HMSO, 1989.

18 *Building Bulletin 7: Fire and the design of educational buildings,* sixth edition. ISBN 0 11 270585 5. HMSO, 1988.

Further reading

HMI publications

Education Observed series:

Special needs issues: A survey by HMI
ISBN 0 11 270722 X. HMSO, 1990.

Information technology and special educational needs in schools: A review by HMI
ISBN 0 11 270729 7. HMSO, 1990.

Implementation of the Curriculum Requirements of the Education Reform Act series:

National Curriculum and special needs: Preparations to implement the National Curriculum for pupils with statements in special and ordinary schools, 1989–90
ISBN 0 11 270776 9. HMSO, 1991.

HMI Reports:

A survey of provision for pupils with emotional/behavioural difficulties in maintained special schools and units 62/89

Educating physically disabled pupils 110/89

Effectiveness of small special schools 279/89

Special needs and the National Curriculum 1990–91: A report by HM Inspectorate
ISBN 0 11 270795 5. HMSO, 1992.

The Design Notes, broadsheets, Architects and Building Branch Papers and HMI Reports referred to in this document are available free of charge from:

Department for Education
Publications Centre
P O Box 2193
London E15 2EU

Tel. 081-533 2000